"Building strong relationships with great mentors is essential to any professional's success. But approaching a mentor can be intimidating. Omadeke will take you by the hand and walk you through a step-by-step process of how to do this in a way that will enrich your life and your mentors. Remember, you are not asking for help—you are asking a person to make a wise investment in you, one that will leave your corner of the world a better, less lonely place."

—**Kim Scott,**
Best-selling author of *Radical Candor*

"*Mentorship Unlocked* is the book I wish I had at the start of my career. Janice Omadeke effectively demystifies the otherwise elusive nature of mentorship. Drawn from her own experience and extensive research, this is a practical guide to finding and working with mentors that will help you grow. It helped me rethink my own role as a mentor.

—**Chris Hyams,**
CEO of Indeed

"*Mentorship Unlocked* is a practical guide with tangible advice everyone can use to get the most value from a mentoring relationship."

—**Shellye Archambeau,**
Author of *Unapologetically Ambitious*

"*Mentorship Unlocked* is your go-to guide for navigating the changing world of mentor-mentee relationships in today's work environment. Written by one of Austin's most impressive entrepreneurs who is literally the global thought-leader in this all-important practice of mentoring, this book is packed with personal stories, practical tools, and useful examples that show you how to make meaningful connections without losing your true self. Whether you're climbing the corporate ladder, carving out a creative niche, or starting your own thing, *Mentorship Unlocked* has got your back in helping you hit your goals and find success."

—**Hugh Forrest,**
Chief program officer, SXSW

"*Mentorship Unlocked* is an extremely insightful and comprehensive guide to tapping into mentorship as an invaluable resource for career building. Whether you're a mentor, mentee, or both, Omadeke's fascinating anecdotes and precise, thorough analysis makes *Mentorship Unlocked* an engaging and thoughtful page-turner. This book is a must-read for anyone and everyone who wants to build fruitful professional relationships."

—**Liz Elting,**
Best-selling author of *Dream Big and Win*
and Founder and CEO of the Elizabeth Elting Foundation

"In *Mentorship Unlocked*, Janice Omadeke vividly brings to life the link between mentorship and growing career confidence. It's an insightful read for professionals looking to make bold, strategic bets in their careers. The book's blend of real-life examples and strategies is empowering and enlightening."

—Selena Rezvani,
Best-selling author of *Quick Confidence:
Be Authentic, Boost Connections,
and Make Bold Bets on Yourself*

"As I reflect on my own journey, I can attest to the transformative power of mentorship. The guidance and wisdom shared by mentors played a pivotal role in shaping my business. *Mentorship Unlocked* resonates deeply with those carving their own path in the business world. Its sincere, focused content provides the tools needed for creating strong mentor relationships. An invaluable read for anyone aspiring to reach new heights in their career."

—Kendra Scott,
Founder, Kendra Scott

"Mentorship helps make any career more satisfying and rewarding. *Mentorship Unlocked* provides the wisdom and tools to cultivate meaningful and productive relationships between mentors and mentees—and help both parties grow."

—Scott Sonenshein,
Best-selling author of *Stretch*
and coauthor of *Joy at Work*

"*Mentorship Unlocked* is like a coffee chat with a trusted mentor, tailored for women entrepreneurs. It's approachable, blending personal experiences with practical strategies. No matter where someone is in their career, this well-crafted work enables leaders to engage their entrepreneurial instincts to shape mentoring strategies aligned with who they really are."

—Jan Ryan,
Serial entrepreneur, board advisor

"*Mentorship Unlocked* offers a refreshing, mindful approach to building career relationships. It skillfully navigates the complexities of today's work environment with a focus on personal growth and awareness. A must-read for anyone seeking a meaningful career journey."

—Chip Conley,
Founder and CEO, Modern Elder
Academy, and best-selling author

"*Mentorship Unlocked* reflects the truth that 'people will be what they can see.' It's a modern and refreshingly honest book, offering practical and relatable mentorship insights any can follow. This book is a valuable tool, guiding real people towards real goals with strategies that work from beginning to end."

—Joseph Kopser,
Serial entrepreneur, investor, start-up advisor

MENTORSHIP UNLOCKED

MENTORSHIP UNLOCKED

THE SCIENCE AND ART OF
SETTING YOURSELF UP FOR SUCCESS

JANICE OMADEKE

WILEY

Published by John Wiley & Sons, Inc., Hoboken, New Jersey.
Published simultaneously in Canada.

For general information on our other products and services or for technical support, please contact our Customer Care Department within the United States at (800) 762-2974, outside the United States at (317) 572-3993 or fax (317) 572-4002.

Wiley also publishes its books in a variety of electronic formats. Some content that appears in print may not be available in electronic formats. For more information about Wiley products, visit our web site at www.wiley.com.

Library of Congress Cataloging-in-Publication Data is Available:

ISBN 9781394243228 (Cloth)
ISBN 9781394243235 (ePub)
ISBN 9781394243242 (ePDF)

Cover Design: Wiley
Cover Image: © Adeijsha Brown
SKY10067058_021424

To the three wisest women I'll ever know:

My sister for paving the way for generational growth.

My aunt, Martha, for embodying a loving and gracious heart.

My mother, Lorena, for being the shoulders we had the privilege to stand on to reach new heights.

Contents

About the Author

JANICE OMADEKE IS a pioneering serial entrepreneur who made a life-altering decision when she transitioned from her role as a corporate graphic designer to embark on a journey into tech entrepreneurship. As a remarkable achievement, Omadeke stands as Austin's first Black woman to secure a venture-backed tech exit in 2022, and she ranks among the first 100 Black women to raise over $1 million in seed funding for her first tech company.

Omadeke is the exited CEO and founder of The Mentor Method, an enterprise software designed to drive transformative change within company cultures through the power of mentorship. Guided by her belief in data-driven decision-making as a cornerstone for strategy, innovation, and cultural transformation, she has honed this model through over a decade of leadership experience within Fortune 500 companies. Her roster of influential clients includes Amazon and the US Department of Education.

Omadeke earned recognition as one of *Entrepreneur* magazine's 100 Women of Influence in 2022. Her voice and commitment to mentorship and entrepreneurship can be found in publications such as *Forbes*, the *Harvard Business Review*, *Fast Company*, *The Austin Business Journal*, *Black Enterprise*, and *Inc.* Omadeke was part of a select group of diversity and inclusion leaders chosen to participate in the 2016

White House Summit on Building the Tech Workforce of Tomorrow. Alongside her entrepreneurial expertise, she holds a PMP (Project Management Professional) certification and has received a certification in Entrepreneurship from MIT.

With a unique blend of directness and compassion, Omadeke is dedicated to making a positive impact. Her approach is both strategic and heartfelt, always driven by a deep sense of intention. Beyond her professional pursuits, you can find Janice cooking, reading, taking on a self-development project, or a combination of the three.

Introduction

RAISE YOUR HAND if this sounds familiar:

- You work hard and are successful by most societal measures, but something feels missing.
- You don't feel that your professional life and larger purpose are connected to each other.
- You regularly think about switching careers or starting a business but don't know how to pinpoint your niche and needs.
- You often feel as though you don't have anyone to turn to when you need advice, honest feedback, or a new perspective.
- You have received a lot of advice about work and career, but none of it really resonates with you and your circumstances.

The above resonated with me in my career, too. I came to a realization. Despite a successful career, I felt something was lacking in my professional life. I had progressed through the ranks at a Big Four management consulting firm and several leading defense contracting companies, successfully managing projects for billion-dollar clients, including government agencies. My career took off through strong creative leadership and implementing tactical solutions that attracted and retained customers. I significantly contributed to profitability, from winning multimillion-dollar accounts to overhauling internal

systems to cut costs. My educational journey led me to MIT for entrepreneurship and Harvard for strategic management, studying alongside
some of the brightest minds globally. At the heart of my journey was a
missing element: my own identity. My early career was driven by the
pursuit of financial success and climbing the corporate ladder, often
neglecting deeper introspection. This mindset was shaped by the times
and my background. Launching my career amid the rise of tech giants
and evolving work cultures, I was swept up in a narrative of relentless
ambition, often sidelining self-reflection. As a Black woman and a
first-generation American, the weight of expectations left little room
for anything but achievement.

It took nearing burnout to compel a profound reassessment of my
career and life goals. This introspection revealed how important the
role of my community served in both my success and my pursuit of
what lay ahead. Finding mentors who truly resonated with my experience was challenging, but once found, they were instrumental in my
growth as a professional and individual. Mentorship provided me with
emotional and mental wellness in the workplace, fostering resilience
and sustainability.

Mentorship, I've learned, is more than guidance; it's a nurturing
process that enhances our mental and emotional well-being by sharing
professional wisdom and encouragement. It's this holistic approach
that makes mentorship a key factor in workplace success.

Mentorship nurtures our mental and emotional well-being, enriching our professional lives through shared experiences, expertise, and
encouragement. That's why mentorship helps us become more successful at work.

This impact is mirrored in the experiences of leading companies and
business figures. Employees engaged in mentoring programs are promoted five times more often than those without a mentor. Serving as a
mentor also correlates with career advancement—those who serve as a
mentor are six times more likely to be promoted to a higher position.[1]

That's just one example of the power of mentorship. Mentorship is
important for the future of work and leadership, too. According to a
survey by CNBC, millennial and Gen Z professionals with a mentor
are 21%–23% more likely to report being satisfied with their current
job compared to those without a mentor. *Harvard Business Review* finds

that people of all ages who served as mentors experienced lower levels of anxiety and described their job as more meaningful than those who did not mentor. They also found that 89% of those who have been mentored say they'll go on to mentor others.[2] The feeling of belonging, lower stress, and deep relationships tie directly to employee retention.

However, there's a noticeable disconnect between the recognized value of mentorship and how few people access it. A significant percentage of professionals acknowledge mentorship's importance, yet a much smaller number actively participate in such relationships. Even fewer establish clear objectives within these mentorships. Olivet Nazarene University surveyed 3,000 professionals on mentorship. They found that 76% of people think mentors are important, but only 37% had one. Of those who had mentoring relationships, only 41% had formal goals for the mentorship.[3]

In 2017, I started my first company, The Mentor Method, a platform dedicated to creating genuine mentor-mentee connections based on shared passions and interests, moving beyond traditional job roles or network-based matches. I was inspired by my strong belief in the power of mentorship, reinforced by my personal experiences. My focus was on forming powerful professional relationships that significantly alter work and life perspectives.

My journey with The Mentor Method marked significant milestones, including becoming the first Black woman in Austin to achieve a venture-backed tech exit and one of the first 100 Black women to raise over $1 million in venture funding in the US. In 2022, I was honored by *Entrepreneur* magazine as one of 100 Women of Influence. These achievements showcase the profound importance of mentorship across various stages of life, career, and entrepreneurship. Mentorship is instrumental in providing support, building skills, expanding networks, and helping achieve goals.

The success I've achieved in my career is largely due to the time, effort, and guidance invested in me by my mentors. My approach to seeking mentors was proactive, data-driven, and systematic, driven by a deep curiosity about the dynamics of successful mentorship. I observed a common trend: many navigate their path to success in isolation.

One reason for this is the lack of mentorship investment in many corporate environments. Additionally, conventional business wisdom often doesn't align with modern realities. Common archetypes such as the lone wolf or verbally abusive tech genius dominate the narrative, focusing on individual triumphs rather than the power of community. An entire industry of content has been developed to help you change yourself to become a singular success—not on building the community you need to thrive.

It's harder to stand out in a crowd when the majority of your team is working from home, there are fewer networking events, and people slowly step away from a culture of fear-based over-functioning in favor of a more self-advocating approach to a career lifestyle. We are inundated with career and mentorship advice from every medium and platform, telling us we earn mentors and advance in our careers by changing who we are, not by following our inner voice.

Add to that how the way we work has changed in recent years— hybrid and virtual work has been accelerated thanks to the pandemic. Before the pandemic, 61% of mentor relationships occurred naturally.[4] Although how we work has changed for so many, the need for mentors remains as important as ever, but the changes in the way we work means how we bring mentors into our lives has changed as well. Organic mentorship, what is oftentimes viewed as the "ideal" mentorship structure, can be more challenging to establish if you spend most of your days working within the four walls of your home and through your computer screen. There are fewer opportunities to interact with potential mentors in person—chance meetings on the elevator or standing in line for a sandwich in the cafeteria, for example.

In writing this book, my goal is to offer distinct career guidance to learn, apply, and advance swiftly through specialized career advice that accelerates learning and advancement. It's about becoming complete individuals without fearing judgment or adhering to outdated professional standards. You're encouraged to adopt an entrepreneurial mindset in your career, relevant whether you're in a corporate, creative, or entrepreneurial role. Remember, mentorship is a key tool for you to achieve your goals.

Work is a significant driver in our lives, and considering the time we spend working or thinking about work, our careers greatly influence our quality of life. The various "isms" that affect us at work, particularly women of color, make our professional journeys crucial indicators of our overall well-being.

Mentorship is an empowering form of self-advocacy, helping you break through barriers to achieve the life you've envisioned.

Bringing Entrepreneurial Thinking to Your Career

As CEO and founder of The Mentor Method, I advised numerous executives to adopt an entrepreneurial mindset for employee retention. I emphasized the importance of treating staff retention with the same urgency as revenue and customer loss. I advocate for professionals to actively shape their careers, seeking roles that offer personal satisfaction, not just societal approval. Mentorship is needed in this journey, acting as a compass for career advancement.

My own shift from corporate roles to entrepreneurship taught me the value of entrepreneurial thinking in all professional contexts. I viewed my corporate career as my first business. I focused all of my energy on reaching a six-figure salary and paying off my student debt within the first five years of my career. This mindset parallels starting a business: I was the product, corporations were my customers, and my salary was the revenue.

Embracing entrepreneurship in your career means fighting for what you want. If you've ever stretched resources, fought for a raise, or handled unpaid emotional labor, you possess an entrepreneurial spirit.

So how do we leverage our entrepreneurial instincts to find the right mentor and mentor others? I believe the whole process starts from within.

Who am I?

What do I want to get out of mentorship?

What strengths can I share with someone else to help them advance?

What type of lifestyle do I want in the future?

What does a fulfilling career look like for me and the overall life I want to achieve?

I advise everyone to start by answering these key questions before strategically pursuing one of the most important relationships in a career.

This approach goes against traditional career advice. Successful mentorship isn't about getting others to like you; it's not about conforming or fitting into a predefined mold. Contrary to old advice, your innermost feelings about work and career aspirations are important. Our souls, our true selves, do matter. In my earlier career, when I followed the prescribed mold, mentor relationships felt forced, shallow, and uncomfortable. I didn't learn as much as I could have because I didn't feel comfortable with that person. And if I didn't have a clear idea of who I was and what I wanted out of that relationship, how could they even help me?

> Contrary to old advice, your innermost feelings about work and career aspirations are important. Our souls, our true selves, do matter.

Ignoring our own instincts can lead us to unfulfilling careers. This book guides you in using intuition to find mentorship that honors your true self. While mentors can help refine our approach, it's important to distinguish this from losing one's identity. I once strived to fit the "professional boss babe" image, but it took a toll on my well-being. This book will help you break this cycle, advocating for authenticity over conformity.

Before You Begin - What to Know Before You Get Started

In the chapters that follow, I outline a strategy that anyone can use to create, build, and deepen mentorship relationships to achieve your goals. I want you to walk away from this book with a focused strategy and the exact steps to find the right mentors, feel confident and empowered as a mentor, guiding mentees and deliver excellent mentorship, and use both as tools to help you achieve the professional goals of your dreams.

There are a few things I want you to know before you start reading the rest of the book:

First, let's correct a widespread misconception: mentorship isn't reserved for the newcomers in the professional world. Whether you're just beginning or you're an experienced professional seeking fresh avenues for growth, mentorship is a recurring need as we navigate through changes and gain clarity on our career paths. Despite common narratives focusing on the youth, mentorship transcends age. Leaders at the top of their industries also seek counsel and new learning opportunities. Your mentorship needs may shift with your career progression, but the value it adds remains. This book will assist anyone in unlocking their potential and stepping into their leadership role, complete with engaging exercises and reflective prompts.

> *This book will assist anyone in unlocking their potential and stepping into their leadership role, complete with engaging exercises and reflective prompts.*

Second, we will focus on helping you build your action plan, with the intention that you will come back to it many times over the course of your career. I'll provide insights and tools to empower you to develop a well-defined mentorship strategy that will lead to tangible results in your career and in your overall well-being. By implementing the insights and tools offered in these pages, you'll gain the confidence to navigate the science and art of mentorship with ease and efficiency.

Third, we'll focus on the cornerstone of all your relationships: yourself. We'll begin by acknowledging the unique talents and capabilities you contribute. Recognizing your true self beyond societal constructs is a profound act of self-love. We'll discuss how genuine engagement with your career can lead to both success and satisfaction. We'll examine aspects of your personality that influence your work and future, harnessing your strengths to redefine leadership. A key resource in this process is a mentor, helping you refine your discoveries and build a fulfilling career.

This book isn't about escaping your current situation through overwork, nor does it suggest mentorship as a substitute for personal effort. It's about tapping into and optimizing the potential within you. We'll address everything from mentorship basics to the spectrum

> *This book isn't about escaping your current situation through overwork, nor does it suggest mentorship as a substitute for personal effort.*

of mentors beneficial at various career stages, including transitional periods. For entrepreneurs, we'll address specific mentorship strategies for company growth. I'll encourage a wide-ranging panel of mentors to provide a comprehensive perspective on your career, moving beyond a narrow, prescriptive approach.

My hope is that you'll find an opportunity for self-reflection in these pages. I hope you distance yourself from limiting ideas about who you can be at work. I hope you use the tools to build a plan that you can implement immediately. I hope you learn that the very specific practice of mentorship in professional spaces is valuable no matter what you do for a living.

1

Laying the Foundation: The Parallels between Mentorship and Entrepreneurship

EVA* WORKED IN the corporate world for over five years and was now making a comfortable salary. She had worked hard to get where she was, but something was missing. Her career felt more in the hands of her circumstances than something she felt she was driving. She felt stuck, frustrated, and unfulfilled. Eva knew she had the potential to do more, but she wasn't sure how to get there.

Eva's story is not uncommon. Many professionals who have reached a certain level in their careers find themselves in a similar situation. They are successful by most measures, but they feel like something is missing. They want more out of their careers, but they aren't sure how to get there.

Eva could binge-read articles on mentorship and career advancement written by people who have not struggled to find mentors, go to countless networking events, get burnt out, and let a scarcity mindset or feeling overwhelmed convince her to stay on her path of solo career navigation. Or she could make five times her salary over her career by learning how to be efficient and effective at finding a series of

---

*Working with my clients and hearing your stories is deeply rewarding. Out of respect, some names have been changed in the examples throughout this book to protect privacy, but these are real examples.

strategically timed mentors using the same guiding principles found in entrepreneurship.

For Eva, her frustration stemmed from a lack of direction. She had worked hard to climb the corporate ladder, but she wasn't sure where she wanted to go from there. She felt as if she was just going through the motions and that her career had plateaued. She wanted to do something more meaningful, but she wasn't sure what that was.

As I've spoken with professionals like Eva, companies that want to keep their talent, my entrepreneurial peers, and entrepreneurs I've mentored or invested in, I noticed a common thread in the mentorship world and entrepreneurship world: finding a mentor is a lot like the early stages of building your company.

If you skipped the introduction to dig into the heart of the book (I do the same thing), I encourage you to read it, as I explain the parallels of being the CEO of your career in greater detail in the introduction. This chapter is a brief overview of the key leadership skills top CEOs embody for success that will help you as you take on a leadership role in your career and journey to meet powerful mentors, before starting to reflect on your internal identity in the following chapters.

How an Entrepreneurial Mindset Pays Off in the Long Run

Let's compare the journeys of two aspiring entrepreneurs on their quest for success. Person 1, eager and self-reliant, embarks on this journey solo. In contrast, person two recognizes the value of mentorship and seeks guidance from an experienced mentor.

Both individuals start their careers with similar roles and salaries. However, person 2, guided by their mentor, consistently hones their skills, tackles challenges more effectively, and capitalizes on growth opportunities. This mentorship-supported path leads them to excel in their current role and positions them strategically for future success.

On the other hand, person 1, navigating their career independently, faces a more challenging learning curve. The absence of a mentor's wisdom means they might struggle to showcase their full potential and compete for promotions. Over time, the gap between the two becomes evident.

The moral of the story? Mentorship can be a game changer, providing valuable insights and guidance that pave the way for personal and professional triumph. The statistics paint a clear picture. Those who engage in mentoring experience a remarkable fivefold increase in promotion rates compared to their non-mentored counterparts. Additionally, a noteworthy 25% of mentees report a salary increase, a striking contrast to the mere 5% among those not involved in mentoring.

Embodying Your Role as the CEO of Your Career Path

Finding a career mentor and embarking on an entrepreneurial journey share striking parallels, illuminated by the common thread of core leadership skills they demand. Both pursuits require a deep sense of initiative, driving individuals to actively seek growth opportunities. Just as an entrepreneur takes the initiative to build a business from the ground up, finding a mentor demands the initiative to seek guidance that can catalyze personal and professional development.

> *Just as an entrepreneur takes the initiative to build a business from the ground up, finding a mentor demands the initiative to seek guidance that can catalyze personal and professional development.*

Both endeavors involve risk-taking as a fundamental ingredient. Both career mentorship and entrepreneurship require a willingness to embrace risk-taking. Entrepreneurs often venture into uncharted territory, making bold decisions to realize their vision. Similarly, seeking guidance from a mentor involves stepping out of one's comfort zone and trusting the mentor's insights to shape your path forward.

Adaptability is a cornerstone skill that bridges the worlds of mentorship and entrepreneurship. In an ever-evolving landscape, both mentors and entrepreneurs must navigate change and unpredictability using what they know to be true and meet them with curiosity to challenge their thinking to reach the next level. The ability to adapt to shifting circumstances, whether it's pivoting business strategies or incorporating new insights from a mentor, defines the success of these journeys.

Problem-solving skills are invaluable assets in both contexts. Entrepreneurs confront challenges head-on, devising solutions to complex issues that arise along the way. Similarly, the mentorship journey can present mentees with hurdles, and the mentor's role extends to guiding them in developing effective problem-solving strategies.

Resilience serves as the backbone of success in both mentorship and entrepreneurship. Entrepreneurs must persevere through setbacks, failures, and uncertainties, while mentees benefit from the resilience to continue seeking guidance despite potential rejections. This shared tenacity drives growth and transformation in both scenarios.

Lastly, passion fuels the heart of both endeavors. Entrepreneurs infuse their ventures with passion, the driving force behind their innovations and dedication. Similarly, mentees who approach mentorship with a genuine passion for growth and learning unlock the full potential of their relationship with mentors.

Whether navigating the corporate world with a mentor's guidance or forging an entrepreneurial path, the qualities of initiative, risk-taking, adaptability, problem solving, resilience, resourcefulness, and passion brings together the pursuit of success in both journeys. Embracing these skills not only fuels personal growth but also drives the realization of goals, both as a mentee on a career journey and as an entrepreneur on a quest for innovation and impact.

The Enduring Rewards of an Entrepreneurial Approach

Applying entrepreneurial skills in a corporate career can significantly enhance the process of finding a mentor and accelerate the journey toward personal and professional growth. I'll use the first five years of my career as an example.

My initial encounter with the "entrepreneur of my own career" concept was a personal journey that began within my own professional trajectory. Unbeknownst to me at the time, my role as a corporate graphic designer bore a striking resemblance to entrepreneurship. My singular focus was directed toward achieving a six-figure salary and repaying student loans within the initial five years of my career. To draw parallels between my career and entrepreneurship, I viewed myself as the product, corporations as the customers, and the revenue took the form of salary increments and finding fulfilling workplaces. This dual perspective, combined with my personal experiences, instilled in me a profound understanding of the similarities that extend into mentorship and how it can propel career advancement.

Early in my professional journey, a particular job left me disheartened and confined. I faced challenges within my team's culture, grappling with pressure to conform and struggling to navigate the corporate landscape as someone from a diverse background whose race, gender, and lack of network made me stand out compared to my peers. Despite my inner turmoil, I hesitated to voice my concerns, echoing the advice I had received from previous supervisors about embracing the status quo. As I sought guidance through an array of articles, a recurrent theme emerged: the importance of ongoing education. Recognizing the value of translating my creative skills into tangible business applications to become an asset to business development teams, I chose to engage in entrepreneurship courses at MIT.

One part of the program proved particularly relevant—the intricacies of establishing a company's foundation for market entry and validating core assumptions. The curriculum covered customer identification, locating target audiences, product definition, pricing strategies, and more. Adapting the exercises to my situation, I channeled my need for a new job into the business model. This approach created a new way of seeing my career, leading to transformative results, and changing my career within a 10-month span.

Employing entrepreneurial principles to craft a meaningful career, enhance my quality of life, and prioritize well-being allowed me to pinpoint specific companies aligned with my aspirations. Through this process, I identified the critical role of mentors and support systems in my journey. The mentors I encountered, who you will learn more about throughout the book, played instrumental roles in refining my portfolio and shaping my career narrative. Together, we outlined my aspirations, pinpointed relevant job listings through specialized websites, and refined my interview preparation.

With their personalized guidance, I secured a position at a prominent management consulting firm that perfectly matched my aspirations down to the type of manager I reported to and projects I worked on. This role was more than a job; it embodied inclusivity, invigorating work, inspirational leadership, and a strong emphasis on mentorship as an integral part of the firm's culture.

In summary, my journey to bridge the gap between entrepreneurship, career mentorship, and personal growth began as academic exploration. Over time, it transformed into a revitalizing life journey, a groundbreaking entrepreneurial endeavor, and a powerful tool we now wield to amplify your own career pursuits.

◻   ◻   ◻

Ultimately, the management of your career is in your hands. The most influential entrepreneurs in history harnessed their strengths to revolutionize their fields through creativity, problem solving, and unwavering dedication. These traits, along with resilience and self-belief, are accessible to anyone willing to embrace them. In the upcoming chapters, we will explore various strategies to empower you in your career journey and on the path to connecting with the ideal mentors. As we proceed, the next chapter will focus on the foundational resource in your future mentor relationships: yourself.

2

The Inner Compass: Guiding You to Outstanding Mentorships

IN OUR RELENTLESS pursuit of career success, we often overlook the most important aspect that can lead us to extraordinary mentorship opportunities: understanding ourselves. Embracing who we are, acknowledging our strengths and quirks, and aligning with our values and goals can significantly enhance our ability to find mentors who genuinely connect with us. This chapter explores the transformative power of self-awareness and its profound implications in shaping fulfilling mentorship relationships.

> *Note: Mental health is a core aspect of well-being for everyone, regardless of their profession. In this book, we will specifically focus on self-understanding and self-awareness, recognizing that mental health encompasses various dimensions. It's important to clarify that this book does not concentrate on therapy or therapist-based support. If you or someone you know is seeking professional therapeutic assistance, please access the best available resources for those needs. Our focus here is to explore how self-awareness and self-acceptance can empower you in your career and mentorship journey.*

Exploring Your Inner Landscape

Growing up, I was never exposed to the idea of therapy or the importance of emotional depth in both my personal and professional life.

In my family and pre-30s community, seeking therapy was seen as a last resort, reserved only for those facing serious emotional struggles. I was taught to rely on religion, hard work, and the wisdom of our elders to guide me through life.

As I ventured into my corporate career, my focus was solely on achieving goals and making progress. I never took the time to consider *why* that was the goal, if it was a goal I actually wanted, or what reaching that goal would empower me to do. The idea of introspection and self-awareness seemed secondary to the demands of the fast-paced business world. Conversations about emotional intelligence, empathy, or inclusion were absent from the dialogue. I followed the prescribed path outlined by my company's performance review plan, adhered to societal "nice girl" expectations, and worked diligently to build a successful resume without considering whether my career choices aligned with my higher purpose in life. I was a corporate racehorse—sprinting down the track because I was told to, without having an understanding of where exactly I was going, how fast to get there, and not knowing who entered me into the race, to begin with.

> I was a corporate racehorse— sprinting down the track because I was told to, without having an understanding of where exactly I was going, how fast to get there, and not knowing who entered me into the race, to begin with.

For the first nine years of my professional life, I remained unaware of who I truly was. I put little thought into my work style, communication preferences, or even my energy levels throughout the day. My career journey was governed by external influences, leaving my true self obscured by a veil of conformity. Deep down, I knew the companies I worked for, the cultures established, and the people I was expected to be mentored by were all incompatible with my natural alignment. I fought it until I became so fed up that I created a company to avoid the situation altogether and ensure others never experienced similar feelings either.

Tapping into Self-Insight: Unearthing Inner Strengths

It wasn't until I reached a critical juncture in my career that I recognized the value of self-awareness for stronger leadership. Initially, I was resistant to unpacking who I am because I thought, "How could I be the youngest manager in the history of one of the top management consulting firms if I don't know myself? I know I'm smart, I know I'm driven, I know I'm an incredible graphic designer with a strong portfolio and student loans I want to pay off in the next two years. What else do I need to know?" However, as I further explored the concept, I realized its transformative potential.

In my early 30s, I decided to explore the concept of self-discovery. I sought therapy as a means to understand myself better—my goals, desires, and the kind of life I aspired to lead. I attended therapy sessions every other week, working with an exceptional therapist who gently guided me through the process of self-exploration.

Through this process, I discovered that I had been suppressing my intuition, overlooking its invaluable guidance in my decision-making. Moreover, I realized that my sense of worth was heavily tied to my career success, leading me to neglect other aspects of my life that were equally important.

For example, I am an extroverted introvert. I enjoy meeting new people and reconnecting with colleagues while also enjoying the bliss of being home at the end of the day. I am a morning person and am up at 5 a.m. on weekdays (thank you, my dear friend, routine morning anxiety), and my brain starts getting to work by 5:30 a.m. By the end of the workday, I like immediately getting home to unwind two or three days a week to save energy for weekend errands and plans with friends. I neglected this need and would attend 10–12 networking events per week because that's what "real entrepreneurs" did to get ahead. I didn't get a large return on that time, and by the end of the week, the interactions were tense and uncomfortable because I was neglecting myself. When you're not in alignment with who you are, you risk facing the same thing.

Transforming Your Professional Self

I needed mentors who aligned with my values and strengths, allowing me to flourish both personally and professionally. This realization was an epiphany. It highlighted the need to embrace my genuine self and seek mentors who understood and appreciated me for who I truly was. This newfound clarity allowed me to identify office dynamics that energized and motivated me while filtering out those that drained my energy. Consequently, I developed a deeper network of mentors, friends, and colleagues who genuinely supported and understood me.

> *The impact of embracing my true self was remarkable. Career opportunities that resonated with my passion and values emerged more frequently.*

The impact of embracing my true self was remarkable. Career opportunities that resonated with my passions and values emerged more frequently. I found myself fueled by an enthusiasm that I hadn't experienced before. My overall well-being improved, as did the quality of my relationships with others.

Embracing Your Professional Identity

Understanding your professional identity is the foundation on which authentic mentorship is built. It involves gaining clarity on your work habits, learning style, strengths, areas of improvement, and how you prefer to communicate. By knowing yourself deeply, you'll articulate your needs to potential mentors confidently and make informed decisions when selecting mentors.

Start by exploring your work style. Are you someone who thrives in a fast-paced environment, or do you prefer a more methodical approach? Understand your communication preferences, whether you prefer written correspondence, phone calls, or face-to-face meetings. Identify your peak energy hours and learn to leverage them for optimal productivity. Recognize your strengths, those unique qualities that set you apart and drive your success. Acknowledge areas for improvement, as they represent opportunities for growth. Consider the types of teams and managers that bring out the best in you. Reflect on the missions that resonate with your values and inspire your dedication. Evaluate whether a strong sense of purpose in your workplace is essential to you. Clarify your priorities and aspirations, both within your career and beyond, to strike a balance that brings fulfillment to all aspects of your life.

Tools to Help You Find Your Professional Identity

Oftentimes assessments are used to help your manager understand who you are without asking probing questions or making assumptions. You can use the results of your assessments to get a deeper understanding of who you are, decide which parts feel true and which ones don't, and see how you can use that information to start crafting your professional identity.

Such assessments will give you an overview of your results; details on what makes you unique, strengths, and areas you may want to improve; and information on how you operate on teams. There are three assessments I've used across my career that may be helpful for you: the CliftonStrengths Assessment, the Enneagram, and the Human Design assessment.

The CliftonStrengths Assessment categorizes your unique talents into 34 CliftonStrengths themes. It measures your natural thinking, feeling, and behavioral patterns and provides insights into managing potential weaknesses. It helps you discover your inherent strengths, develop them, and use personalized results and reports to support your personal and professional growth.

The Enneagram is a personality framework that explores the motivations, desires, and fears of nine distinct personality types, offering a detailed and specific understanding of individual behavior tendencies.

Human Design provides you with insights into your decision-making processes, motivation, and energy management. It is a unique approach to understanding one's personality, emotions, and energy centers. It explores how individuals are wired to make decisions, collaborate within teams, and navigate various aspects of life.

Combining assessment results offers a multifaceted and comprehensive view of your personality, helping you create a deeper understanding of yourself and your professional identity. By integrating the insights from the assessments you choose, you can gain a more holistic view of who you are, both personally and professionally. This understanding allows you to make informed decisions about which aspects of yourself you want to nurture and develop further. It provides clarity on which skills to focus on, and it empowers you to navigate your professional journey with a sense of self-assuredness, knowing how you're wired and what truly inspires you.

Unmasking Your Potential: Your Superhero Origin Story Unfolded

As a fan of comic books, I've always been intrigued by the pivotal moment when a superhero in the story discovers their purpose. It's that life-altering instant that defines their path forward and keeps them motivated even on the darkest days. They become intimately connected with their mission and purpose. This kind of connection can be helpful to find within yourself because, just like a superhero's journey, your career will have its highs and lows, especially when you're on the path to find mentors. On those challenging days, you'll need something to hold onto, a reminder of why you're putting in all of this effort. So what fuels your motivation? What's the deep driving force behind your desire to seek mentors and advance in your career?

So what fuels your motivation? What's the deep driving force behind your desire to seek mentors and advance in your career?

In my case, my origin-story moment occurred when I tragically lost my mother to pancreatic cancer in 2018. It was during that difficult time that I received a clear message about the path I needed to follow for the years ahead. This revelation led me to seek mentors who could help me achieve those goals, including honing my soft and tactile skills.

Recognizing your own origin-story moment can help you identify your core values and provide your mentor with a deeper understanding of your perspective. I've shared mine in conversations with mentors, and it has offered more insight into my motivations than any LinkedIn profile ever could.

Your moment doesn't have to be as emotionally charged as mine was. Back in my early corporate days, my motivation for seeking mentors was quite practical: I wanted to increase my salary to escape the situation of sharing a home with four roommates. Having a structured and organized living space is something I consider essential, and the chaos created by living with four people was entirely counter to that need. The origin-story moment in this scenario was rather common. It was the frustration of discovering that my roommate had finished the last of my peanut butter at a time when I needed to stretch my next paycheck. In that exasperating moment, I firmly decided: "I can't keep going like this. This is causing me too much stress. I need to find a different job that pays better."

Or perhaps your origin-story moment is a deep-seated passion for a specific field, driving you to gain expertise and ensure a lasting impact in that domain. Whatever it may be, embrace it with honesty, as it's the driving force behind your journey to mentorship and career advancement.

Navigating with Precision

Drawing a parallel to ordering a meal, imagine two people exploring dinner options through the same meal delivery service. Person 1 browses through the available choices without a clear idea of what they truly want or need. They spend a considerable amount of time deliberating, unable to make a satisfying decision. On the other hand, person 2 approaches the task with a clear understanding of their dietary preferences, allergies, and taste preferences. As a result, person 2 quickly selects a restaurant that offers the perfect meal for them, saving time and avoiding frustration.

In the same vein, knowing yourself with more clarity as you meet mentors streamlines the process. Clarity about your professional identity empowers you to confidently articulate your needs to potential mentors, make informed decisions when selecting mentors, and build strong and mutually beneficial mentorship relationships more efficiently.

Understanding Compatibility

Understanding the types of people who energize and recharge you is equally needed when seeking a mentor. There's nothing more challenging than trying to be mentored by someone whose personality doesn't align with yours. We all have our pet peeves, and recognizing them, along with the personality and values traits that make you feel comfortable and ready to connect, is a critical step in finding the right mentors. By being aware of these aspects of yourself, you can easily identify who is and isn't a good fit for a mentor relationship. Just like any meaningful friendship or positive interaction, that initial chemistry with a mentor is vital. It doesn't necessarily mean they need to have the same personality as you but rather one that you find easy and enjoyable to be around. If you find yourself focusing on how much you dislike their personality, you might not fully benefit from the mentorship.

The journey to finding the right mentors starts with understanding and accepting oneself. This introspective process empowers individuals to articulate their professional identity more clearly and confidently. Understanding ourselves is a fundamental journey that shapes our lives and careers in profound ways. Embracing our authentic selves and seeking mentors who appreciate and support our uniqueness can lead to transformative experiences.

Embracing our authentic selves and seeking mentors who appreciate and support our uniqueness can lead to transformative experiences.

The pursuit of authentic mentorship begins with knowing and accepting who we are, paving the way for a fruitful and fulfilling mentorship journey. Prioritizing self-awareness is the key to unlocking the doors to exceptional mentorship opportunities that align with our true selves.

Managing Burnout While Exploring

Burnout is something we all experience at some point. It manifests differently in each person. You might find yourself easily tired, less motivated, or perhaps you become more irritable. Whatever the signs, check in with yourself if you start feeling burned out while exploring mentorship opportunities. The mentorship journey should be an enjoyable and enriching process, not something that drains your energy and affects your overall well-being. If you feel burnout creeping in, take a step back, give yourself a break, and come back to it when you feel ready and recharged. This journey should be fulfilling, and taking care of yourself along the way is an essential component of its success.

Managing Any Pressure in the Process

Embarking on the journey to find a mentor can feel like a high-pressure undertaking, especially for my fellow perfectionists. It requires vulnerability and self-awareness, in addition to the pressure of striving for your career goals within a certain time frame if you set one. Understandably, you care deeply about your career and want to form meaningful connections, which can make the process feel intense. It might be tempting to choose the first potential mentors you encounter, especially if you feel a sense of urgency about your career.

When you start to feel the pressure mounting, take a moment to do a self-advocating check-in. Remember that you deserve a great network of mentors, and you are actively putting in the effort to find them. You are the CEO of your career, and whatever the outcome, you will be okay. Keeping this in mind will help you remain calm and confident throughout your mentorship journey.

> *You are the CEO of your career, and whatever the outcome, you will be okay. Keeping this in mind will help you remain calm and confident throughout your mentorship journey.*

Instead of approaching mentorship as a "hunt," consider adopting an "exploring" mindset. Think about your encounters with potential mentors and the spaces you enter as curious explorations. Imagine yourself on an adventure of discovery rather than feeling pressured to find a perfect match. This perspective takes the pressure off and allows your true personality to shine through.

We've all been in a high-pressure sales situation, where the sales associate is clearly under pressure to try to meet their monthly quota. Their pushiness and anxious energy might make you wary and less likely to become their customer. Similarly, the energy you bring to your interactions with potential mentors matters. Just like encountering a pushy salesperson who gives off uneasy energy, being too focused on the outcome can create a similar effect in your encounters with potential mentors. By adopting an exploring mindset, your authentic personality will shine through, making connections more genuine.

As you venture into potential mentor "watering holes," view it as a journey of exploration. You are simply curious to see whether there are potential mentors in these communities, whether they align with your goals and values, and whether your mentor persona hypotheses you developed in Chapter 4 hold true. Not every encounter will lead to an immediate mentorship opportunity, but each interaction provides valuable insights about yourself and the type of mentor you're seeking. If you attend a group and don't find immediate mentor options, that's okay. It's not a wasted effort; it's an opportunity to learn and refine your preferences. Every lesson learned is a step forward, never a setback.

Every lesson learned is a step forward, never a setback.

By maintaining an exploring headspace, setbacks won't shake your self-confidence or trust in the process. You'll bounce back and feel equipped to try again. Remember, entrepreneurship and mentorship share similarities—the path to success is rarely straightforward or easy. It involves learning, strategic thinking, and resilience.

The best CEOs know that reaching their goals takes adaptability and perseverance. As you explore potential mentors as the CEO of your career, embrace the lessons you learn along the way. Each experience will provide valuable insights, guiding you closer to finding the right mentor for your journey.

Each mentor serves a unique purpose and may be more relevant at different stages of your career. In my own experience, I didn't connect with certain types of mentors until four or five years into my career. Trust the timing of these encounters instead of feeling rushed to check all the boxes.

Exercise: Identifying Your Mentorship Goals and Personal Growth

In this section, we'll stay curious and explore some thought-provoking questions that will help you gain clarity on your mentorship goals and understand yourself better. Treat this as your personal mentorship workbook, and jot down your answers and reflections. Let's get started:

1. Why do you want a mentor right now?
   Reflect on your current career situation and what you aim to accomplish in the near future. Are you looking for guidance

to navigate a career transition, looking to enhance your communication skills, or aspiring to take on more leadership responsibilities? By identifying your specific goals, you'll be better equipped to find a mentor who aligns with your objectives.

Example: "I want a mentor right now because I'm transitioning to a leadership role at work, and I need guidance on effective leadership practices. Additionally, I feel the need for a fresh perspective to help me identify blind spots I may take with me in my new role and develop strategies to work through those gradually."

2. What are you hoping a mentor will help you solve?

Consider the challenges and obstacles you face in your professional journey. Is it difficulty with networking, managing stress, or navigating office politics? By pinpointing your specific challenges, you can articulate what support you hope to receive from a mentor, making the mentorship relationship more targeted and effective.

Example: "I'm facing difficulties in managing my workload, and I hope my mentor can provide insights on how to prioritize my time effectively so I have more time to meet with friends. I also want guidance on navigating office politics and building strong relationships with my colleagues when I don't feel like I align with the culture."

3. Reflect on your personal strengths and areas for improvement.

Self-awareness is a powerful tool for personal growth. Take some time to honestly evaluate your strengths and areas where you have room for improvement. Consider both technical skills and soft skills such as communication, leadership, and adaptability. This reflection will help you identify what you can bring to the mentorship relationship and where you might need guidance.

Example: "My strengths include strong problem-solving abilities, email or written communications, and excellent project management skills. However, I believe I could improve my public speaking and assertiveness in team meetings."

4. Have you fully assessed your inner environment?

Examine your personal and professional relationships and the impact they have on your growth and well-being. Identify the people who uplift and inspire you, as well as those who may bring negativity or hinder your progress. By creating a support-ive and positive environment, you'll be better prepared to engage in fruitful mentorship experiences.

Example: "I've realized that some friendships at work drain my energy and focus on office gossip rather than professional development. To create a more positive environment, I will limit my interactions with these people and seek out colleagues who share my passion for growth and collaboration."

5. How will you track progress and accountability?

Establish clear, measurable goals for your mentorship jour-ney. Determine how you will track your progress and hold your-self accountable for your development. Whether it's setting milestones, maintaining a journal, or seeking feedback from your mentor, tracking your growth will empower you to make the most of the mentorship opportunity. We will go into more detail on building a "mentor tracker" and how to manage meet-ings with your mentor in Chapter 6.

Example: "I will set quarterly goals related to my leadership development, and I'll schedule regular check-ins with my men-tor to discuss my progress. Additionally, I'll keep a journal to record my reflections and track the insights gained during our mentoring sessions."

This exercise is all about *you* and *your* growth. Be honest, open, and willing to explore new perspectives. As you complete these exer-cises, you'll gain valuable insights that will empower you to find the best mentors and start on a transformational mentorship journey. Keep your answers and reflections in a place where you can easily return to them throughout your process, revisit and update them as your goals change, and build on them as you develop your mentorship plan throughout the course of the book.

In the next chapter, we'll explore the core of mentorship, what exactly mentorship is, and how to apply this self-awareness to pinpoint the most suitable mentor for both your short-term and long-term career objectives. The self-awareness exercises will serve as valuable tools, as in the next chapter we explore locating mentors who can expertly guide you toward the ideal match for your professional advancement and personal growth.

3

Essential Mentorship Principles for All

In my research, I uncovered a common perception surrounding mentorship—it's often viewed as a privilege reserved for those with the right connections or working in mentorship-friendly organizations. Surprising statistics show that 71% of executives choose to mentor individuals who share the same gender or race. Considering that 76% of CEOs are white and represent a significant majority among top executive officers, this pattern presents a substantial challenge.[1] Mentorship can be accessible to everyone, irrespective of their background or network. It's a critical way to level the playing field, especially for aspiring professionals with great ambition but limited access to extensive networks. To address this issue, I've developed a new mentorship definition that is inclusive and supportive of all individuals seeking guidance and growth in their careers.

I define mentorship as follows:

Mentorship is a positive and collaborative partnership between two individuals, where one person (mentee) wants to learn from the experiences of another person (mentor), with the goal of using that knowledge to excel in their own career. Whether it's aiming for a promotion, exploring a new career path, transitioning careers, or pursuing something truly unique, the mentor's role is to guide the mentee on the best path toward their goal while staying true to the mentee's core identity. Drawing from their own lived experiences and relevant anecdotes from others, mentors provide insightful guidance to help mentees make informed decisions and unlock their full potential during the mentorship journey.

This relationship can take various forms—short-term or long-term, formal or informal—depending on the specific needs and availability of both the mentee and the mentor, offering flexibility and tailored support for each individual seeking mentorship.

Having a mentor with different experiences and perspectives can help you grow and think outside of the box. Don't limit yourself to mentors who are just like you.

While it can be helpful to have a mentor who has been through similar experiences, it's not necessary. In fact, having a mentor with different experiences and perspectives can help you grow and think outside of the box. Don't limit yourself to mentors who are just like you.

Studies have proven mentorship is a key tool to achieving a fulfilling career. Across multiple studies, the following results stand out:

- In mentoring programs, 25% of mentored employees experienced salary grade changes, compared to just 5% among nonparticipants.
- Mentees are five times more likely to receive promotions, while mentors have six times higher promotion rates. Notably, 89% of individuals with mentors eventually become mentors themselves.
- Diversity, equity, and inclusion (DEI) mentorship programs are credited by 80% of employees for fostering inclusivity, skill development, and sponsorship. Additionally, 89% of those with mentors feel a greater sense of value and appreciation from their colleagues.
- Ninety-seven percent of individuals with mentors express the value of these relationships, with 87% of those in mentoring programs finding empowerment and increased confidence. For 84%, mentoring relationships serve as a source of inspiration for both mentor and mentee.[2]

What Mentorship Is and Isn't

Mentorship is:

- **A safe space for vulnerability:** Mentorship offers a safe and non-judgmental space for mentees to express their vulnerabilities, fears, and aspirations, fostering a supportive environment for personal development.

- **A relationship based on empathy:** Mentorship involves mentors who demonstrate empathy and understanding, actively listening to their mentees' concerns and providing empathetic guidance to address challenges effectively.

- **A tool for building self-confidence:** Mentorship helps mentees build self-confidence, empowering them to embrace their unique strengths and leverage them to overcome obstacles and seize opportunities.

- **A gateway to industry insights:** Mentorship provides mentees with valuable industry insights, helping them gain a deeper understanding of the current landscape and trends while also staying ahead of emerging developments.

- **A platform for skill development:** Mentorship offers mentees an opportunity to acquire new skills, knowledge, and expertise from experienced mentors, empowering them to enhance their capabilities and excel in their chosen fields.

- **A relationship built on trust and mutual respect:** Mentorship is founded on trust and mutual respect between mentors and mentees, fostering an environment where open communication and honest feedback thrive.

- **A journey of continuous learning:** Both mentors and mentees engage in a journey of continuous learning, exchanging ideas, perspectives, and experiences, leading to personal and professional growth for both parties.

- **A means to broaden networks:** Mentorship enables individuals to expand their networks by connecting with professionals from diverse backgrounds and industries, opening doors to new opportunities and collaborations.

Fun and engaging: Mentorship can be a fun and enjoyable experience as mentors and mentees collaborate, share experiences, and celebrate achievements together.

A launching pad to success: Mentorship serves as a launching pad for success, propelling mentees toward achieving their goals and aspirations while also providing a platform to explore new opportunities.

Mentorship isn't:

Transactional: Mentorship is not a transactional exchange where only one party benefits from the relationship. It goes beyond a mere quid pro quo, emphasizing the growth and development of both the mentor and mentee.

An instant fix: Mentorship is not a quick fix for all career challenges. It requires time, effort, and commitment from both parties to build a strong and sustainable mentor-mentee relationship.

One-size-fits-all: Mentorship is not a one-size-fits-all solution. Different individuals have unique needs and goals, so mentorship should be tailored to suit the specific aspirations and circumstances of each mentee.

Limited to a specific age group: Mentorship is not exclusive to certain age groups. It can be beneficial at any stage of one's career, from early professionals to seasoned experts, fostering growth and learning across generations.

A substitute for personal responsibility: Mentorship is not a replacement for the mentee's responsibility in shaping their own career and life. It's a supportive relationship that empowers the mentee to take ownership of their decisions and actions.

About the mentee becoming the mentor: Mentorship is not about turning the mentee into an exact replica of the mentor. It's about nurturing the mentee's unique strengths and helping them embrace their individuality.

Guaranteed overnight success: Mentorship is not a guarantee of instant success or rapid career advancement. It involves consistent effort, dedication, and perseverance over time.

Limited to in-person interactions: Mentorship is not confined to in-person meetings. It can take place through various platforms, including virtual meetings, emails, phone calls, and social media, providing flexibility in communication.

The Types of Mentorship Dynamics

There are four primary types of mentorship dynamics: peer-to-peer, traditional, reverse, and group.

Peer-to-peer mentorship represents a collaborative relationship between individuals at similar career stages, allowing them to mutually support each other's professional development. For instance, two junior engineers working together, providing feedback, and aiding each other in their work exemplify this dynamic.

Traditional mentorship, on the other hand, involves an experienced professional guiding and supporting a less experienced mentee, typically in a one-on-one format. For instance, a seasoned accountant may mentor a junior accountant, helping them navigate their career growth and offering insights into the industry culture and expectations. While this book predominantly focuses on traditional mentorship, the strategies outlined here can be adapted to various mentorship dynamics. It's essential to tailor your approach to what best suits your unique career path.

Reverse mentorship offers a distinct approach where someone earlier in their career mentors a more experienced individual. This approach benefits senior professionals seeking insights into emerging technology or current market trends from younger generations. For instance, a seasoned professional might be mentored by someone earlier in their career, providing expertise in mastering social media and navigating its nuances.

Group mentorship involves multiple individuals congregating within a supportive setting, all sharing a common goal of professional growth. In group mentorship, a mentor often facilitates discussions, provides feedback, and steers the collective toward their shared objectives. An example of group mentorship is a professional working group for new mothers returning to the workplace. In this scenario, they exchange experiences and receive guidance on their new normal while navigating their careers.

Overall, each type of mentorship offers unique advantages and disadvantages, and it's important to select the approach that best aligns with your goals and values.

What to Look For in a Mentor

In Chapter 2 we discussed the importance of mentee-mentor compatibility. One of the most important things to look for in a mentor is a similar alignment in values. If your mentor doesn't share your core values, it's going to be difficult to build a strong and lasting relationship. You want to find someone who is communicative, supportive, emotionally available, open-minded, and well networked. These qualities will help you to build more connections and navigate your career more effectively.

The most impactful mentors are often the ones who, like you, didn't plan their career based on fame but received a level of visibility because of their authenticity, approachability, and dedication to the work that lights a fire in their souls.

It's also important to pay attention to the impact that your mentor can make on your actual career rather than your ego and social media presence. The most impactful mentors are often the ones who, like you, didn't plan their career based on fame but received a level of visibility because of their authenticity, approachability, and dedication to the work that lights a fire in their souls.

When choosing a mentor, it's important to trust your gut. How do you feel around this person? Do you feel anxious or judged, or do you feel comfortable talking to them about things that aren't working out the way you planned? If your gut tells you to avoid someone, listen to that more than paying attention to what magazines they've been featured in.

Roles and Responsibilities of Mentors

Trusting your gut on who to work with as your mentor gets easier when you know what to look for. While everyone is different and will bring a unique experience to the mentor relationship, there are core roles and responsibilities you should feel confident your mentor will be able to bring to the table. These include:

1. Providing guidance and support: One of the primary roles of a mentor is to provide guidance and support to their mentees. They help mentees navigate challenges and provide advice on how to achieve their goals.

2. Sharing expertise and knowledge: Mentors are typically more experienced than their mentees and are expected to share their knowledge and expertise in their field of work.

3. Providing feedback: Mentors provide constructive feedback to their mentees on their performance, behavior, and skills.

4. Encouraging self-reflection: Mentors encourage their mentees to reflect on their experiences and help them develop self-awareness.

5. Challenging their mentees: Mentors challenge their mentees to step outside of their comfort zones and take on new challenges.

6. Setting goals and creating action plans: Mentors work with their mentees to set goals and create action plans to achieve them.

7. Being a role model: Mentors lead by example and model behaviors and values that they expect their mentees to emulate.

8. Providing networking opportunities: Mentors introduce their mentees to their professional network and provide opportunities for them to make new connections.

9. Advocating for their mentees: Mentors advocate for their mentees and help them navigate organizational politics.

10. Maintaining confidentiality: Mentors should maintain confidentiality and respect the privacy of their mentees.

Your turn: What mentorship myths are holding you back from finding your mentor?

The Difference between a Mentor and a Coach

Mentorship and coaching are important tools in your professional development, but they are not interchangeable terms. Each role has its unique characteristics and responsibilities.

A mentor is an experienced and trusted advisor who provides guidance, advice, and support to a less experienced person. Mentors typically have more experience and knowledge than their mentees and help them develop their skills, knowledge, and abilities in a particular area. Mentors may provide both personal and professional guidance and help their mentees navigate their careers.

A coach, on the other hand, is someone who helps a person improve their performance in a specific area. Coaches help people set goals, develop strategies to achieve those goals, and provide feedback and support to help them improve. Coaches typically work with people on a short-term basis and focus on specific skills or competencies. Coaches charge a monthly retainer or charge per session and may have packages for a set number of sessions you can purchase to work with them.

For example, Dominique, a mid-level manager at a fast-growing law firm, found the perfect balance in her professional journey by having both a mentor and a coach. Her mentor is a senior partner at the firm, who offers invaluable guidance on long-term career strategy, provides insights from his own journey, and helps Dominique navigate the complexities of the legal world. On the other hand, her coach, Tim, specializes in coaching professionals on time management and stress reduction techniques, which are needed in the demanding legal environment. Tim helps Dominique refine her skills, set specific goals, and manage her daily tasks effectively. With her mentor's guidance, she is building a solid foundation for her legal career, while Tim's coaching enables her to tackle daily challenges with precision and resilience. The combination of mentorship and coaching has become a dynamic support system that propels Dominique forward in her role as a mid-level manager in the fast-paced law firm.

Working with both a mentor and a coach can be an invaluable pairing, as the mentor is personal and career-focused, and the coach serves as a diagnostic test you can use to have deeper discussions with your mentors.

How Many Mentors Should You Have?

The number of mentors you should have depends on your goals and aspirations. I often receive questions about the ideal number of mentors, and I find that having more than three active mentors at a time can be quite challenging. While having multiple mentors is possible, it's important to strike a balance. Establishing and maintaining mentor relationships requires time, energy, and intention. Considering your personal life and commitments, limiting the number of mentors you actively engage with can be immensely valuable.

Think of your mentors as a diverse set of resources meant to help you develop a holistic view of your career and improve your quality of life, each playing a specific role in guiding your life's direction. It helps you avoid putting the pressure on one specific mentor to be everything for you throughout the journey of your career life span. Over time, it's beneficial to add these recommended mentors to your network of mentors:

> *Think of your mentors as a diverse set of resources meant to help you develop a holistic view of your career and improve your quality of life, each playing a specific role in guiding your life's direction.*

1. Company insider;
2. Skill master;
3. The money-minded mentor;
4. The industry mentor;
5. The network mentor;
6. The influential ally; and
7. Peer mentor.

Let's take an in-depth look at each mentor type.

Company Insider

This mentor understands the inner workings of your company and can provide guidance on company culture, politics, and how to navigate the organization to achieve your goals. Sixty-one percent of mentees stated that their mentor works at the same organization.[3]

Top Three Characteristics:

- Deep understanding of company culture: Possesses a deep understanding of the organization's structure, culture, and dynamics, allowing them to offer valuable insights and advice.
- Political savviness: They can guide you through the intricacies of office politics, helping you navigate the organization effectively and build strong relationships with key stakeholders.
- Knowledge of organizational structure: This mentor can provide firsthand experiences and anecdotes from their time within the company, offering you real-life examples to learn from.

Pros	Cons
Valuable company insights: Their knowledge of the organization can offer valuable insights that others might not be aware of, giving you a competitive edge.	Limited external perspective: Their focus might be primarily on internal matters, potentially overlooking broader industry trends and practices.
Tailored guidance: They can provide customized advice specific to your company's culture and structure, helping you adapt and succeed.	Conflicting interests: They may have a vested interest in your success within the company that doesn't align with your interests if you seek to leave the company in the near future, which could influence their advice.
Access to opportunities: An insider mentor can introduce you to growth opportunities within the company, such as special projects or cross-functional teams.	Risk of bias: In some cases, an insider mentor may have biases that could affect their guidance.

Navigating the intricacies of a company's environment requires insights that go beyond the surface. As you engage with your mentor, who is deeply entrenched within the company, it's important to have a set of intentional questions to draw on. These questions will not only help you gain insights into their experiences but also allow you to harness their expertise to navigate challenges and embrace opportunities.

Here are some questions you can consider asking your company insider mentor:

- How do you recommend effectively showcasing my skills and contributions to ensure they are recognized by both colleagues and higher-ups?
- Could you share any instances where you've seen innovative ideas come to life within the company? What factors contributed to their success?
- As someone who has observed the company's growth over time, what trends do you foresee shaping the industry, and how is the company preparing to respond to them?
- Are there any specific professional development opportunities within the company, such as training programs or workshops, that you believe would benefit my growth?
- Could you share insights into how to strike a balance between taking calculated risks to innovate and adhering to the company's existing processes and practices?
- What strategies do you suggest for fostering strong cross-functional collaborations and building a network across different departments and teams within the organization?
- What strategies have you found successful in building strong relationships with key stakeholders?
- Could you provide examples of challenges you've faced within the organizational structure and how you overcame them?
- How do you recommend staying adaptable in a rapidly changing work environment while still aligning with the company's long-term goals?
- How do you stay updated on the changes and developments within the company? Are there any sources you recommend for staying informed?
- In your experience, what are some unwritten rules or norms within the organization that newcomers might not be aware of?
- Could you share stories of how you've seen individuals advance within the company? What common traits or actions contributed to their success?

- Are there any specific growth opportunities, teams, or projects you would recommend I explore to further develop my skills and career within the company?
- How do you balance your commitment to the company's goals with your own professional aspirations?
- Have you ever encountered situations where the company's direction conflicted with your personal values or beliefs? How did you handle it?

Skill Master

This mentor has expertise in a specific skill or area, such as public speaking, project management, or networking, and can help you develop those skills to advance your career. They may or may not work at the same company.

Top Three Characteristics:

- Expertise in a specific skill: A skill master excels in a particular area, such as public speaking, project management, or even knowing spreadsheet equations, and can share their knowledge to help you enhance these skills.
- Strong communicator: They excel at explaining complex concepts and providing actionable feedback, helping you improve and refine your abilities. They possess strong teaching skills, enabling them to impart their expertise to you effectively.
- Continuous learners: Skill masters are continuously learning and growing themselves, setting an example for you to strive for ongoing improvement.

Pros	Cons
Skill enhancement: Their expertise can significantly enhance your professional abilities, making you more competitive in your field.	Limited scope: Their guidance might be limited to the specific skill they excel in, overlooking other areas needed for overall career growth. Limited guidance on broader career strategies.

Pros	Cons
Career advancement: Developing specialized skills can open doors for promotions and new career opportunities.	Skill relevance: If your mentor's expertise becomes outdated, it might not align with current industry demands.
Versatility: Skill masters can be valuable across various industries and roles, as their guidance is skills-focused.	May not understand your overall career goals: If the skill master is too focused on the skill itself, they might provide advice that is too focused on skill development and not enough on other aspects of your career progression.

As you engage in mentorship with a skill master, asking the right questions can unlock insights that enhance your proficiency and career trajectory. Here are a few questions to consider asking your skill master mentor:

- How do you recommend integrating the specific skill you excel in with other aspects of my professional strengths to create a well-rounded skill set?
- What industries find this skill the most valuable long-term?
- How can I effectively measure my progress and growth in this skill over time? Are there specific benchmarks or metrics to track?
- In your experience, what strategies or techniques have helped you stay up-to-date and continuously improve your expertise in [specific skill] despite evolving industry trends?
- Could you share any personal anecdotes or challenges you faced while developing your expertise? How did you overcome them, and what lessons did you learn along the way?
- As the professional landscape evolves, how do you stay updated and ensure your expertise remains relevant in the face of changing trends and demands?
- Considering the rapidly changing landscape of our industry, how do you suggest balancing the mastery of a specific skill with the need to adapt to emerging technologies and practices?
- Beyond honing the skill itself, how can I effectively showcase and leverage my proficiency in [specific skill] to advance my career and seize new opportunities within our organization?

The Money-Minded Mentor

This mentor can help you navigate salary negotiations, strategize for promotions, and provide valuable insights into succeeding in your professional journey, as it relates to your salary or building a sustainable personal finance model for your preferred lifestyle.

Top Three Characteristics:

- Negotiation skills: The money-minded mentor excels in negotiation and can guide you in salary negotiations, promotions, and other career advancements.
- Strategic planning: They can help you devise a long-term career strategy, setting realistic goals and milestones for financial growth. They possess a strong understanding of financial matters and can help you make strategic decisions regarding your career trajectory.
- Non-work-related financial insights: The money-minded mentor is knowledgeable about financial management, investments, and wealth building that can help you navigate income-building opportunities that align to your long-term financial goals.

Pros	Cons
Salary and compensation boost: Their guidance can lead to improved salary packages and benefits, maximizing your earning potential.	Singular focus: Their expertise is primarily related to financial aspects, potentially overlooking other essential career development areas.
Financial security: Learning about financial planning and investments can help you secure your financial future.	Varying goals: Individual financial goals might differ, and the mentor's advice might not align with your personal aspirations.
Career road map: They assist in creating a clear road map for career advancement, considering both short-term and long-term financial goals.	Risk aversion: They may lean toward conservative approaches, which could hinder risk-taking and innovative career moves.

Engaging with a mentor who is well versed in financial matters can provide you with valuable insights into strategically managing your career growth and financial well-being. To make the most of your mentorship with a money-minded mentor, consider asking the following questions:

- Could you share your experiences with successful negotiation strategies for salary increases or promotions? How can I effectively apply these strategies to my own career advancement?
- In addition to traditional compensation, what alternative avenues have you explored for generating income or creating financial opportunities? How can I explore these options for myself?
- In developing a long-term career strategy, what factors should I consider to ensure alignment between my professional goals and financial aspirations? How can I create achievable milestones for financial growth?
- Could you provide examples of how your financial decisions have positively influenced your career trajectory? How can I incorporate similar decision-making into my own career path?
- Given the dynamic nature of the job market, what steps can I take to enhance my financial security while pursuing ambitious career goals?
- What resources, books, or courses do you recommend for gaining a deeper understanding of personal finance and wealth-building strategies?
- As I progress in my career, how can I ensure that my financial goals and strategies evolve alongside my changing responsibilities and opportunities?
- In your experience, how have you seen financial decisions impact career trajectories? Are there specific examples where strategic financial planning led to significant advancements?

The Industry Mentor

This mentor will provide valuable insights and guidance specific to your industry or professional field. They will help you navigate industry trends, challenges, and opportunities, enabling you to stay ahead in your career and make informed decisions. Of people with a mentor, 81% said that their mentor works in the same industry.[4]

Top Three Characteristics:

- In-depth industry knowledge: An industry mentor possesses extensive knowledge of trends, challenges, and opportunities specific to your professional field.
- Networking opportunities: They have a well-established network within the industry, providing you access to influential contacts and potential collaborators.
- Insider insights: The industry mentor can offer insider insights into best practices, technologies, and developments in your field.

Pros	Cons
Industry expertise: Their guidance ensures you stay current with industry trends and remain competitive.	Limited perspective: Their knowledge might be limited to a specific industry, potentially neglecting cross-industry insights.
Relevant career guidance: They offer tailored advice relevant to your industry, streamlining your career trajectory.	Niche expertise: Industry mentors may not be as versatile as skill-based mentors, focusing mainly on their field of expertise.
Access to opportunities: The mentor's network can lead to exciting opportunities, including partnerships, speaking engagements, or industry-specific projects.	Geographic constraints: Their insights might not apply universally if they are region-specific mentors.

An industry mentor brings a wealth of in-depth knowledge and a well-connected network to your mentorship journey. To make the most of your mentorship experience, consider asking the following questions that highlight the expertise and experiences of your industry mentor:

- Given your extensive industry knowledge, could you share some insights into the current trends and emerging opportunities that professionals in our field should be aware of?
- How do you recommend I connect with influential individuals or potential collaborators within our industry?

- Could you share a recent industry trend or development that has caught your attention? How do you see this trend shaping the future of our field?
- Are there any industry-specific events, conferences, or online communities you recommend for expanding my knowledge and networking circle?
- In your experience, what are the most valuable skills or certifications that professionals in our industry should focus on to stay competitive in the job market?
- In your experience, what are some effective strategies for overcoming challenges that are common in our industry?
- As our industry evolves, are there any skills or areas of expertise that you believe will become increasingly valuable for professionals like me?
- Could you share a personal career anecdote where you had to adapt to a major industry shift? How did you navigate the change, and what lessons did you learn from that experience?

The Network Mentor

Networking is essential for career growth, and this mentor can assist you in expanding and nurturing your network connections.

Top Three Characteristics:

- Vast network: This mentor has an extensive and diverse network of professional connections across various industries.
- Relationship-building skills: They excel at building and maintaining strong, meaningful relationships with their network.
- Connector: A network mentor actively connects individuals in their network who can mutually benefit from collaboration.

Pros	Cons
Networking opportunities: They can introduce you to valuable contacts within their extensive network, broadening your reach.	Time constraints: Network mentors with busy schedules may have limited availability for regular mentoring sessions.

(*Continued*)

Pros	Cons
Interdisciplinary insights: A diverse network exposes you to ideas and perspectives from various fields, fostering innovation.	Superficial connections: The vastness of their network might result in more superficial connections, lacking depth in mentorship.
Skill development: Networking with diverse professionals enhances your communication and interpersonal skills.	Balance: Balancing your time and attention among numerous networking opportunities can be challenging.

The network mentor stands out as a valuable resource for expanding your professional horizons and connections. As you engage with a network mentor, remember to approach your interactions with purpose and curiosity. Here are some thoughtful and insightful questions you can consider asking your network mentor to enhance your mentoring experience:

- How did you build your extensive professional network? Were there specific strategies you found particularly effective in expanding your connections?
- What advice do you have for someone who wants to leverage networking strategically for career advancement? Are there specific types of connections or events you recommend focusing on?
- How do you balance offering value to your network and seeking assistance when needed? Are there certain principles you follow to maintain a mutually beneficial relationship?
- Could you share an example of a collaboration that originated from your network and led to successful outcomes? What key factors contributed to the success of that partnership?
- When it comes to networking events or conferences, how do you make the most of your time and create meaningful connections in a short span?
- Could you provide insights into your approach to maintaining long-term relationships within your network? How do you nurture connections over time?

- In building your diverse network, have you faced any barriers or challenges, and how did you navigate them to create a more inclusive circle?
- Could you share an instance where your network played a pivotal role in solving a complex problem or seizing an unexpected opportunity? How did it unfold?
- What are your thoughts on balancing online networking through platforms such as LinkedIn with in-person interactions? How do you make the most of both approaches?

The Influential Ally

"The State of Allyship Report: The Key to Workplace Inclusion," conducted by Change Catalyst, analyzed the expectations and desires people have from allies, strategies for improvement, and the intrinsic value it holds for business prosperity. The report revealed that 92% of individuals perceive allies as instrumental to their career growth. Furthermore, those who have at least one ally in their work environment are nearly twice as likely to experience a sense of belonging and satisfaction with their workplace culture and job role.[5] Having someone who supports you in spaces where you might face challenges or biases can be incredibly empowering. They use their leadership position to advocate for you among their influential peers and in spaces where their reputation and voice matter to make decisions. In mentorship, celebrating colleagues' achievements, respecting cultural diversity, and aiding career advancement are all hallmarks of being a meaningful ally.

Top Three Characteristics:

- Leadership and advocacy: An influential ally actively advocates for your success and growth within your organization or industry.
- Courageous voice: They use their position of influence to address bias-based barriers and promote inclusivity and diversity.
- Trustworthy support: The influential ally creates a safe space where you can openly discuss challenges and receive valuable advice.

Pros	Cons
Empowerment: Having an influential advocate enhances your confidence and empowers you to pursue ambitious goals.	Dependence: Relying solely on an influential ally may limit your ability to develop self-advocacy skills.
Recognition: Their support can lead to increased visibility and recognition in your professional circles.	Limited availability: Influential mentors often have packed schedules, making consistent interaction challenging.
Overcoming obstacles: The influential ally helps you navigate challenging situations and biases, fostering a more inclusive environment.	Potential conflicts: Your ally's advocacy may create conflicts of interest or raise concerns among others in the organization.

Among the diverse array of mentorship categories, the role of an influential ally holds a distinct position. The following set of questions digs deeper into the attributes and experiences that define an influential ally mentorship. Customize these questions to suit your mentorship journey, and embrace the insights your mentor offers as you navigate your path to success.

- How do you approach advocating for others' growth and success within the organization or industry? Are there specific strategies you find effective?
- Could you share an example of a situation where you used your influence to address bias or promote inclusivity? What outcomes did it lead to?
- What advice do you have for someone seeking to become a more effective ally to their colleagues? How can one navigate the balance between support and empowerment?
- How do you handle situations where your advocacy for someone's growth conflicts with organizational or industry norms? Could you share any lessons from those experiences?
- In your experience, what are some practical ways to build trust with those you advocate for? How do you ensure that your support is genuine and appreciated?

Peer Mentor

A peer mentor is an individual who is in a similar career stage as you and voluntarily offers guidance, advice, and support to help you navigate your professional journey. Peer mentors have recently experienced the challenges and opportunities that you're currently facing, making their insights particularly relevant and relatable. They share their own experiences, provide practical advice, and offer a unique perspective on career growth, skill development, and overcoming obstacles. Peer mentors contribute to your personal and professional development by fostering a supportive and collaborative environment where you can learn from each other's experiences and successes.

Top Three Characteristics:

- Relevance: A peer mentor is just a step ahead of you in terms of career experience, typically with one to three years more experience. Their recent experiences allows them to provide advice and insights that are directly applicable to your current career stage. Peer mentors are closer in career stage, making it easier to relate to their experiences and advice. They understand the challenges and opportunities you face as they have recently navigated similar situations.
- Empathy: Peer mentors possess a strong sense of empathy as they've recently faced challenges similar to what you're encountering. They understand your concerns and can offer genuine support and understanding.
- Accessibility: Peer mentors are approachable and accessible. They understand the importance of being available for discussions, questions, and advice, making them a reliable source of support in real time.

Pros	Cons
Fresh insights: Peer mentors offer fresh insights into the latest trends, technologies, and practices. Their recent experiences can provide up-to-date perspectives that align with current industry developments.	Limited experience: Peer mentors might have limited experience compared to more senior mentors. They may not have faced certain complex situations that a more seasoned mentor could advise on.

(Continued)

Pros	Cons
Realistic expectations: Peer mentors can provide realistic expectations about career progression, work-life balance, and challenges. They offer practical guidance based on their recent experiences.	Competitive dynamics: In some cases, there might be an underlying sense of competition between peers, which could affect the openness and authenticity of the mentorship relationship.
Shared networks: Peer mentors often have networks that are relevant to your career stage. They can introduce you to contacts, events, and opportunities that benefit your growth.	Limited reach: Peer mentors may not have extensive industry connections or access to resources that a more established mentor could provide.

Engaging with a peer mentor can be an invaluable resource for navigating the early stages of professional growth and benefit from firsthand experiences and relatable insights. As you engage with a peer mentor, consider asking the following questions to gain practical advice and guidance tailored to your career stage:

- How did you manage the transition from [your current career stage] to where you are now? Were there specific strategies or approaches that helped you navigate this progression effectively?
- What are some of the most important lessons you've learned during the first few years of your career? Are there any experiences that significantly shaped your professional development?
- How do you balance learning and development while also excelling in your current role? Are there specific resources or approaches you recommend for continuous improvement?
- Could you share an example of a challenge you encountered early in your career and how you overcame it? What insights did you gain from that experience that you can pass on?
- As you reflect on your career journey so far, are there any decisions or actions you wish you had taken differently during the early stages? What advice do you have for avoiding common pitfalls?

Navigating your professional journey often requires more than personal effort. It involves the support and guidance of mentorship from different experiences and perspectives to help you form a holistic view of your career. These mentors bring unique qualities that extend beyond traditional mentorship roles, actively advocating for your growth and success within your organization or industry. Their leadership, courageous voice, and trustworthy support create a powerful dynamic that can significantly enhance your career trajectory.

Navigating your professional journey often requires more than personal effort. It involves the support and guidance of mentorship from different experiences and perspectives to help you form a holistic view of your career.

Putting It All Together

The different mentors will be powerful assets at different points, and it is not a linear process. Here is how each mentor fits to create your network of mentors using the first five years of my first career as a graphic designer:

1. Company insider: In my first six months in the workforce, I sought out a mentor inside the company to help me understand internal politics, how to engage with leadership, and broaden my company-specific network. This person served as my champion to validate my skill set and promotion potential.

2. Skill master: As I was learning about the inner workings of the company overall from my company insider mentor, I focused on learning new design techniques and trends from an art director I met through a design professionals' association to help me deliver marketing materials in a faster time than it was previously taking me. I learned videography from a professional videographer to build my portfolio of skills on my resume.

3. The money-minded mentor: I didn't understand the fine art of salary requirements when I entered the workforce. I was happy to have a job, but I failed to negotiate or do the appropriate research on a salary range based on skill level and being new to the workforce. Once I realized I was underpaid in my second

year in the workforce, and thanks to the advice of an HR manager who worked at another company, I set a goal of reaching a six-figure salary and paying off my student loans within a five-year time frame.

4. The industry mentor: Because my skills mentor was already in the design industry, I sought out a mentor inside the defense contracting industry to help me understand the top companies, key themes in the industry that I should be aware of, the right terminology to use to show a strong understanding of the industry, and market trends. I started pursuing mentors in this category in my third year in the same industry.

5. The network mentor: As an introvert who didn't love networking at the time, I wanted to be efficient with my time by knowing the best three networking groups to join to meet the right people to help me find new career opportunities. I sought out a mentor that loved networking and had a positive reputation to teach me how to build meaningful relationships quickly without burning out my energy, which groups were free but still powerful, and which conferences to attend to maximize connections. This mentor made introductions that helped me get my dream job at a management consulting firm, where I worked for four years.

6. The influential ally: Allyship wasn't a widely discussed concept early in my career, yet I understood that if there was a majority population that was making hiring and firing and promotional decisions, I needed an advocate "on the inside" who could speak to those decision-makers as a peer to ensure I wasn't left out of those discussions. Two mentors did this in two points in the first five years of my career. The first was the head of business development at my first job, who would bring me into business forecasting meetings early to ensure I understood the inner workings of the business; by being connected to him as the reason I was in the meeting, his peers took me more seriously than before. It increased my level of respect and visibility. The second was a creative director in a different department at the management consulting company I worked for four years.

I had interviewed for a role inside her team at the four-year mark of my career but wasn't the best fit. She then introduced me to the creative director in a different department and championed for me to fill a manager role on that team. Her direct advocacy got me the job immediately.

Mentorship emphasizes quality over quantity. Choosing mentors who resonate with your goals and values results in more meaningful and fruitful relationships. As you expand your network, you might find individuals who fit more than one of these categories. Remain open and adaptable in your mentorship search, taking cues from discussions and insights gained over time.

In the upcoming chapter, we'll use your understanding of the diverse types of mentors available from this chapter, to discuss where to find potential mentors, and begin crafting your mentor persona—a preliminary sketch of the qualities and attributes you are looking for as you foster new connections.

> *Mentorship emphasizes quality over quantity. Choosing mentors who resonate with your goals and values results in more meaningful and fruitful relationships.*

4

Finding Mentors and Developing Your Mentor Persona

HAVE YOU EVER felt a brand was tailor-made just for you? That the products or services perfectly matched your tastes, style, and way of speaking? As if they read your mind? This isn't coincidence; it's the result of countless hours spent building customer personas to connect with people just like you. Businesses hire experts to ensure their mission and vision resonate with their ideal customer, and in this case, that customer is you.

Similarly, just like businesses use customer personas to better understand their target audience, a mentor persona can save you time and effort in finding the right mentor. This chapter will guide you through the process of creating a mentor persona and equip you with the tools to discover mentors who feel tailor-made to your needs. The granularity you apply now will pay off in time saved from connecting with unsuitable mentors.

The self-reflection you did in Chapter 2 along with the creation of your mentor persona and the strategies for identifying career mentors who align with your mentor persona are complementary processes. By understanding your strengths, preferences,

By understanding your strengths, preferences, and areas for growth, you can proactively shape the type of mentors you want in your life.

and areas for growth, you can proactively shape the type of mentors you want in your life. For example, if you discovered you have strong analytical skills, excel under pressure, and thrive in small teams within larger organizations, then seeking mentors with these traits or the expertise required to succeed in such environments makes sense. These mentors can become invaluable additions to your mentor persona profile, guiding you along a path that aligns with your unique strengths and career aspirations. In essence, building a mentor persona is about more than qualifications; it's about finding someone who resonates with you both personally and professionally, understands your aspirations, shares your values, and offers guidance tailored to your unique journey. Now, let's start building your mentor persona and unlock the doors to endless possibilities in your professional life.

Why Build a Mentor Persona

Imagine needing someone to help with a kitchen renovation. You know that you don't have the skills to complete the renovation yourself, and watching YouTube videos isn't helping you complete tasks any faster. After a few less-than-ideal do-it-yourself attempts, you begin looking for a company to help you install your new kitchen sink and replace your tiles. You could spend days messaging every company listed in search results without knowing whether or not they specialize in the exact areas you need renovation help, extending your timeline to enjoy your new space and wasting hours talking to the wrong people.

Or you could get specific about your budget, timeline, the type of experience you want the company to have, and when you want to complete the project and only have calls and meetings with companies that are a closer fit with your requirements. By choosing the second option, your likelihood of narrowing your search to find the right company to complete your projects the way you envisioned is much higher. Building your mentor persona will help you similarly by getting specific about the type of person you'd want to have as a mentor.

In earlier chapters, we focused on who you are and what you want to work on. We're now applying what you learned about yourself to look outward at who would be most compatible with you as a mentor and where to find them.

While it might seem that having a broad range of criteria for a mentor will open up more options, it can complicate your search, lead to overanalysis, and make it harder to find the best fit. I learned this lesson early in my corporate career while working at a defense contracting company. The toxic culture of my team was affecting my mental health, and I knew I needed a mentor to help me navigate these challenges and shift to a new industry.

> *While it might seem that having a broad range of criteria for a mentor will open up more options, it can actually complicate your search, lead to overanalysis, and make it harder to find the best fit.*

A mentor persona is a tool designed to foster a meaningful, growth-oriented relationship. The mentor persona helps you pinpoint where to find a mentor and assess whether they are open to the mentoring relationship. The goal is to be specific, detailing where your ideal mentor spends their time, what their interests are, and what type of personality would complement yours.

When I was crafting my mentor persona in my graphic design career, I embarked on a self-reflective journey. I carefully considered where my ideal mentor would spend their time, what their interests might be, and what type of personality would mesh well with mine. This introspective process not only helped me pinpoint my ideal mentor but also provided a deeper understanding of my own goals and aspirations.

Kickstarting the Process: Developing Your Unique Mentor Persona

The first step in crafting your mentor persona is to understand what you want in a mentor. Clarify your objectives, goals, and the specific support you need. Consider the areas where you feel you need guidance, whether it's honing specific skills, overcoming challenges, or navigating career transitions. This introspection will provide you with a clear vision of the qualities and attributes you may want in a mentor.

The key to a good persona profile is starting with broader information and starting to get specific from there. You want to include a range of information to create a comprehensive and detailed profile. The goal is not to create a profile of a real-life person but rather to create a semi-fictional representation that will help you say, "I spotted someone who might be a fit" faster. Here are some key elements to include in a persona profile:

How does your mentor define mentorship? This is one of the most important questions to have nailed down. This isn't about how *you* define mentorship. This is about how your mentor views mentorship because that's how they will interact *with* you. Do they consider mentorship something that's only saved for structured programs inside the company? Do they consider it critical to their own career development?

What excites them about mentoring? When developing mentor personas, identify their specific goals and objectives in the mentoring relationship. Some mentors might be driven by a passion for helping others succeed in their careers, while others seek personal fulfillment through giving back to their community. Understanding their goals enables you to find mentors whose objectives align with your own career aspirations, increasing the chances of a fruitful mentorship.

What are your mentor's areas of expertise and experience? Understanding the mentor's expertise and professional experience will help you pinpoint individuals whose expertise and experiences closely align to what you're seeking to accomplish with a mentor.

What is their leadership style? Although you are different from your mentor, your mentor's leadership style will be a strong indicator of how they will view your leadership journey. It's important to understand their lens on leadership to know where their advice is stemming from.

What are your mentor's behavioral patterns? Mentor personas should include the behavioral patterns that mentors exhibit in their roles. Some mentors may take a proactive approach, offering regular guidance and support, while others might adopt a more hands-off style, encouraging mentees to take ownership of their learning. Some mentors may prefer to only have one mentee per year, while others may want to have several mentees per year with shorter meetings. Understanding these patterns helps you find mentors whose mentoring style complements your preferred approach to learning and development.

What values do you want to share with your mentor? What matters to them? Values play a significant role in mentorship. Mentors with strong values around empowering others, promoting new perspectives, or fostering a growth mindset can create a more enriching mentoring experience where you can bring more of yourself to the table. Identifying shared values builds trust and fosters a deeper connection, enhancing the overall impact of the mentorship. If you're struggling to think of some values, think about the type of leader you want to be, and build based on those. You may also want to find mentors with different values to broaden your knowledge base and awareness of the different types of leaders you may encounter in your professional journey.

How does your mentor communicate? Knowing the preferred communication channels and style of potential mentors sets the stage for effective mentor-mentee interactions. Like any other meaningful relationship you have with another human, the ability to communicate with each other will determine whether the relationship moves forward or not. Some mentors might prefer in-person meetings, while others are comfortable with virtual communication via video calls or emails. Some mentors have a more direct communication style, while others lead with stories and examples first. Understanding these preferences allows you to easily navigate your mentor's communication style, ensuring smooth and productive exchanges.

How does your mentor spend their time outside of work for fun? What are their interests and hobbies? The way someone spends their time outside of work can tell you more about them than what they do for their career. Include details such as what they're passionate about, who they spend their time with, how they start and end their day, and what hobbies they use to recharge. It's unlikely the mentor you connect with will have your exact same hobbies and ways of using their time outside of work. The goal is to learn potential places where you may meet a mentor in a non-work, casual environment, and get a sense of the type of personality that may be a better fit for you. If you meet a mentor who's a strong fit and doesn't have these hobbies, it is not a reason to write them off. It's best to keep an open mind.

What are their professional affiliations? This is about meeting your mentor prospects where they are already spending their professional time to increase your likelihood of meeting the right mentors in a space where they're comfortable and ready to meet you. The business concept for this is "identifying watering holes," which refers to the process of pinpointing where a business's potential customers gather or spend their time. This allows the business to more easily connect with and convert these individuals into paying customers, as they are already in a space where they are open to engaging with what the business has to offer. In your scenario, this looks like the professional affiliations your mentor may be a part of. Networking events, industry conferences, and workshops are excellent avenues for expanding your circle and building meaningful relationships. Do they belong to an association for environmental advocates or a monthly breakfast group for women in tech roles? Creating a list of possible organizations and affiliations your mentor may be a part of will help you get a sense of where you can spend your time, too.

Where are they the most active online? This helps you determine where you may have a chance to reach out to the mentor. Whether that's on a specific social media platform, a virtual book club, or a monthly industry meetup, there are several places your mentor may choose to spend their networking time meeting new people. The goal is to interact in those areas to increase your likelihood of meeting your mentor where they're comfortable and there's a higher likelihood of meeting while also having more to discuss with them if you do engage in a greater conversation in the future.

How do you feel after communicating with them? Your time is equally as important as your mentor's. The energy you put into your mentor relationship is important, and the priority is on you, your career, and the relationships you're developing to create the career you feel good about. Your relationship with your mentor should leave you feeling challenged but still good about yourself. If your mentor belittles you, ridicules you, or makes you feel bad, they are *not* your mentor, and it's best to leave that relationship. Think about how you want to feel after the meetings. Do you want to feel recharged? Do you want to walk away having completed a set of tasks? Do you want to feel understood without tangible takeaways?

What are your mentor's personality traits? Personality traits significantly influence mentorship dynamics. Some mentors might be nurturing and empathetic, providing emotional support, while others might be more results-driven and focused on setting and achieving career goals. By considering personality traits, mentees can find mentors whose coaching style aligns with their needs and preferences.

What not to include:
- Age;
- Number of followers;
- Salary;
- Type of home they rent or own; or
- Superficial details such as their physical appearance.

I used the previous questions to create my mentor personas before I raised seed funding for The Mentor Method. I knew I needed mentors who were experienced in fundraising, could navigate the highs and lows of the fundraising process, and had connections to potential sales and investment prospects. I knew I wanted an outgoing and friendly mentor, and a safe space to make mistakes, test things, pivot, and continue on without judgment. They needed to be involved in multiple entrepreneurship, tech, and diversity-focused groups with a healthy social life outside of work (no work-obsessed pressure, please).

I revised my list multiple times as I tested possible personas and took note of which personas were a better fit than others. Depending

> Each mentor who I connected with by using my personas to first understand and find them had a significant impact on my career.

on the type of mentor I was looking for, some mentors were easier to find than others. Regardless of the time it took to meet them, each mentor who I connected with by using my personas to first understand and find them had a significant impact on my career.

Transforming Your List into a Story

Once you have your list, it's time to turn it into a story that will be easy for you to remind yourself of as you meet potential mentors. Take the details from the list you create and turn it into something tangible you can describe to another person. The goal is to provide enough detail to have the person listening to you say, "Oh, I might know a few people like this."

Example:

My ideal mentor is a serial entrepreneur who enjoys spending time with their children and extended family. Their entrepreneurial experience is diverse, but they have a strong focus on tech and tech-enabled companies that want to scale fast. My ideal mentor had success fundraising for at least one of their businesses and selling at least one business. This mentor is known for their professionalism and ability to make friends wherever they go. They're intentional about attending in-person and virtual pitch events and demo days for early-stage tech companies showcasing underrepresented founders because they hate how these groups are oftentimes left out of the fundraising conversation. They give me room to be my own person while sharing stories of their journey to highlight risks, benefits, and potential outcomes of scenarios I'm encountering at that moment.

Your turn:

Use the previous questions to build your own mentor persona. Stay curious while answering the questions and enjoy the process.

Details such as height, race, and gender identity can be left out to focus on the core values you seek in a mentor. But keep in mind that research indicates that mentoring relationships that are a different gender or race/ethnicity are more likely to provide career benefits, whereas mentoring relationships based on demographic similarity are more likely to provide psychosocial benefits.[1]

Discovering the Right Mentors Who Fit Your Persona

In today's interconnected world, the opportunities to connect with potential mentors seem boundless. If you've already gone through the previous exercises, you likely have a sense of where your ideal mentor spends their time, both professionally and personally.

The Gift of the Virtual World

If you're not particularly fond of attending countless in-person events or if your location lacks the culture and communities you're looking for, consider exploring virtual communities and spaces as a viable alternative. Virtual environments offer a concentrated group of potential mentors with diverse backgrounds and experiences, expanding your likelihood of finding the right match. The key is to be efficient in your search and find the spaces that align with your preferences and goals.

Highly attended virtual events, conferences, and monthly meetups can serve as excellent starting points. Engaging with these platforms provides you with valuable insights into other circles and communities your potential mentors may be part of, thereby expanding your options for exploration. By getting involved in spaces where you feel comfortable and where potential mentors actively participate, you significantly increase the likelihood of connecting with mentors who resonate with your aspirations and can provide valuable guidance.

> *By getting involved in spaces where you feel comfortable and where potential mentors actively participate, you significantly increase the likelihood of connecting with mentors who resonate with your aspirations and can provide valuable guidance.*

Social media presents another avenue for mentorship connections, with LinkedIn as one of the most valuable for your career. This professional networking platform hosts thousands of groups centered on various areas of interest. Let's say you have a specific field in mind, or you aim to break into a particular industry or explore a professional passion in more depth. LinkedIn's group-filtering feature becomes an indispensable tool. For example, imagine you oversee your company's internal communications, such as employee newsletters. In preparation for your upcoming performance review in six months, you are seeking a mentor who understands your current skill set and can assist in your development. By filtering LinkedIn groups focused on marketing professionals, communications experts, and employee engagement, you can join conversations and connect with potential mentors who engage in discussions relevant to your interests.

By thoughtfully exploring these spaces and engaging with mentors in discussions that resonate with your goals, you can significantly increase your chances of finding mentors who will be a perfect fit for your career growth and development.

Exploring Your Current Network and Communities

"Low-hanging fruit" is a concept of personas that businesses use to label sales opportunities that may be easier to get to a "yes" as customers. When it comes to mentorship, "low-hanging fruit" refers to spaces where you're already comfortable and have an existing network. It's natural to gravitate toward familiar faces and rely on your immediate circle when seeking a mentor. This approach has its merits and works for many, but it's important to weigh the pros and cons. Consider the value of tapping into your existing network to connect with potential mentors, and don't overlook the benefits of broadening your horizons by seeking guidance from mentors beyond your current connections.

Exploring your current network to find mentors has several benefits. First, you already have established relationships with these individuals, which can make the mentorship process more comfortable and organic. Trust and familiarity can create a solid foundation for a mentor-mentee relationship, as mentors who know you well and have seen you in professional environments before may be more invested in your growth and development. Second, approaching someone you already know may feel less intimidating than seeking out a mentor from scratch, especially if you're new to networking or mentorship.

Your current network is most likely composed of various groups and affiliations, both professional and personal. Professionally, it may include colleagues, former managers you reported to but no longer work with in any capacity, alumni from your educational institutions, industry peers, or even clients and customers you've interacted with. On a personal level, your network might include friends, family members, acquaintances from social clubs or community organizations, or even friends of friends. These diverse connections can lead you to potential mentors from various backgrounds and expertise.

Using your current network to find mentors also comes with some risks. One concern is the risk of receiving limited perspectives and experiences. It's easy to spend time with people who have a similar belief system as you across multiple areas of your life. If your existing network primarily consists of individuals from a similar industry or background, you may miss out on new insights and fresh perspectives that mentors from different fields could offer. As a result, your personal and professional growth may not reach its full potential.

There's a risk of mentorship blurring the lines between personal and professional relationships. If you choose a mentor who is a close friend or family member, it may be challenging to navigate boundaries and maintain objectivity during mentorship sessions. This could lead to avoiding certain challenges openly to avoid conflict or discomfort with the other person.

To maximize the benefits of using your current network for mentorship, set clear expectations and boundaries from the start. That can include not discussing what you talk about in mentor meetings when you're together for happy hour or among friends, to keep

> *To maximize the benefits of using your current network for mentorship, set clear expectations and boundaries from the start.*

different parts of your relationship separate. Simply stating, "I'm eager to learn from you, but our personal relationship means a lot to me. If we're not in our mentorship sessions, I don't want to talk about work in the same style as our mentorship conversations. I need to know that you'll still see me for who I am outside of that. If you feel that it may change our friendship, I'm okay with not continuing in a mentorship relationship at this time" is enough to set the stage for a boundaries conversation while making your conditions clear in a respectful approach. Transparency and open communication are key to maintaining a healthy mentor-mentee relationship within an existing network.

Keep in mind, seeking mentors outside of your current network offers an opportunity for fresh perspectives, industry insights, and diverse experiences. Expanding your connections can lead you to mentors who challenge and inspire you to grow in new and unexpected ways. While it may require stepping out of your comfort zone, the rewards of finding mentors beyond your existing circle can be truly transformative for your personal and professional development.

Exploring Your Preexisting Work Network

Research shows that 82% of leaders believe that mentoring relationships help foster meaningful connections between mentors and mentees, across departments and the organization.[2] When it comes to finding a potential mentor at work outside of a structured company mentorship program, exploring your current network of coworkers and people you know can be a valuable approach.

These existing relationships can serve as a strong foundation for mentorship and offer unique benefits, but they also come with certain risks that need to be navigated carefully.

One of the key benefits of using your current work network is the familiarity and trust that already exists. Since you have an established rapport with these individuals, it can be easier to initiate conversations about mentorship and express your goals and aspirations.

Much like any other work-based relationship, keeping your personal life out of the discussion is for the best, unless that's the topic you want to discuss with your mentor. Being clear and concise about your skills-based goals is essential when discussing mentorship with colleagues. Communicating your specific areas of interest and the type of mentor you're seeking can help your coworkers identify potential mentors who align with your needs. This clarity can lead to more targeted and relevant suggestions, saving you time and effort in your search.

Seeking mentorship within your current work environment can be positive because these mentors have firsthand knowledge of the company culture, dynamics, and professional opportunities. They can provide insights on navigating internal processes and advancing your career within the organization. Connecting with someone who has successfully navigated similar career paths can be invaluable in gaining a competitive edge among those also vying for similar roles and opportunities.

That said, there are also risks associated with using your current work network to find a mentor. One concern is the potential blurring of boundaries between personal and professional relationships. When a mentor is a coworker or someone you interact with daily, it can be challenging to compartmentalize the mentorship from other aspects of your working relationship. This may lead to discomfort or inhibition in discussing certain issues openly.

If you're planning to leave the company or change departments, it's wise not to mention this during initial conversations about mentorship when you're speaking with someone working at the same company. Sharing these intentions may affect your colleague's willingness to invest time and effort in mentoring you, especially if they see it as a short-term commitment or something that will negatively affect their career as a result.

To mitigate these risks and maintain a professional relationship that also includes mentorship, start by setting clear expectations and boundaries from the beginning. Emphasize your desire to grow and develop within your current role while being open to insights and guidance. Communicate your commitment to the mentorship process and assure your potential mentor that their support will be valued, irrespective of any future career moves. An example of this is, "I like my role at the company, but I'm curious how I can grow my skills to make a bigger impact here. I want to explore that area of my career with you and want to make sure our daily lunch chats don't become a full-time mentorship conversation. What do you think about setting up a time on the first Tuesday of every month to talk about career mentorship and the rest of the time we proceed as usual?"

Exploring your current network of coworkers and people you know at work to find a potential mentor can be a promising strategy. The existing familiarity and trust can create a supportive environment for mentorship to thrive, and mentors from within your workplace can offer valuable insights into company-specific opportunities. Communicate your goals clearly, avoid mentioning plans to leave the company, and set boundaries to ensure a successful and enriching mentor-mentee relationship.

***

Building a mentor persona might seem a bit daunting initially, but once you get comfortable with the process, you'll find yourself applying this in various aspects of your life. Sharpening your focus on the specific qualities you seek in a mentor helps you spot them out of multiple options, saving you from aimlessly searching for mentors that are a fit.

In the next chapter, we will explore the art of engaging with people in the spaces where your mentor personas are likely to be found. We'll also cover how to craft your "elevator overviews," the succinct yet powerful narratives that encapsulate who you are and your career aspirations in a personable way to leave a lasting impression and laying the groundwork for fruitful relationships with potential mentors.

5

Creating a Narrative
That Resonates

AFTER DEVELOPING YOUR mentor persona and starting to attend "watering holes" where your prospective mentors can be found, the next step is crafting a succinct "elevator overview" of yourself. As your vision of an ideal mentor becomes clearer, you'll find it easier to share who you are and the type of mentorship you're seeking. Much like the clarity you gained with your mentorship goals, offering a concise snapshot of your aspirations will allow your network to easily identify potential connections for you. We will focus on constructing 30-second or shorter versions of your "elevator overview." This is most commonly called an "elevator pitch," but for the context of mentorship and protecting your mindset from feeling pressure to "earn" or "win" approval, we're calling it an overview—a clear story about who you are without the expectation of an outcome other than continuing the conversation you're currently in.

Reflect on a skill you excel at, be it professional or personal. At some point, this skill was new to you, and you likely had questions, felt a mix of uncertainty and excitement, and with practice, you not only mastered it but put your unique approach on it to make it your own. The same principle applies to sharing your story. With practice, the process will feel less intimidating and more natural. It's common to resort to emotionlessly rushing through listing facts when telling our stories, but infusing your personality into your narrative can make a significant difference.

By the end of this chapter, you'll be equipped with the tools to share your story with others, and you'll be prepared to approach potential mentors with confidence, secure in the knowledge that you're presenting yourself in the best possible light. Bonus: these overviews can be repurposed to answer the "Tell us about yourself" question during job interviews.

Understanding the Importance

Top CEOs have honed the skill of succinctly describing their business's offerings within 60 seconds, adapting their message to suit the audience they're engaging with to ensure they captivate the listener's attention. This isn't by accident; they collaborate with leadership coaches and experts to weave a compelling narrative that appeals to various stakeholders, from customers to the media.

With a finely tuned "elevator overview," you'll be well equipped to clearly communicate your aspirations and personal story, saving valuable time and maintaining forward momentum in your mentorship process.

Another way to look at it is to picture your overview as the author biography (bio) at the end of an article. In a few lines, writers encapsulate their credentials, expertise, and a personal touch to make them relatable. Crafting such concise yet insightful bios is an art—effectively communicating key points with brevity. And you have the potential to master this art as well.

Crafting such concise yet insightful bios is an art—effectively communicating key points with brevity.

Owning and Embracing Your Strengths, Wins, and Achievements

Downplaying your achievements and using modest language about yourself is often interpreted as a sign of humility and leadership. However, this perception isn't entirely accurate. Constantly undermining your success can inadvertently send a message to your subconscious that your achievements were mere coincidences or that you're undeserving of your accomplishments. This mindset does a disservice to the dedication and effort you've poured into your career. This tendency to self-minimize, unfortunately, is often pressed on women and underrepresented groups, perpetuating a system that discourages them from recognizing and advocating for their worth. Being able to confidently highlight your skills, your strengths, and accomplishments is integral for others to truly grasp your capabilities. Celebrating your achievements isn't about ego; it's about stating truthful details that your audience needs to know to better understand you. Sharing these details, such as your hard-won accomplishments, with others in a way that's grounded in gratitude and authenticity is not just acceptable, but it's a testament to what it's taken for you to reach your current career level.

> *Sharing these details, such as your hard-won accomplishments, with others in a way that's grounded in gratitude and authenticity is not just acceptable, but it's a testament to what it's taken for you to reach your current career level.*

Upgrade Your Introduction: Building a Strong Elevator Overview

I recommend creating two or three versions of your overview to use depending on the amount of time you have with someone. The tone should be true to you. If you're more humorous, infuse your humor into it within reason and still maintain professionalism. If you're extremely passionate about a specific topic, feel free to include that as well.

When speaking to people, you want one that's 30 seconds and one that's 15 seconds, for a shorter conversation; you also want a "double opt-in" written version, used when requesting an introduction to someone you do not know. Each serve different purposes.

Depending on the situation, 9 times out of 10, starting with "Help me find a mentor" will sound transactional and abrasive when the person you're speaking to hasn't offered to help or indicated a giving mindset. If the conversation is flowing and there seems to be a genuine opportunity to mention you're looking for a mentor, include the second portion of the elevator overview details below.

The Key Components of Your Short Overviews

Introduction: Start with a brief introduction, highlighting your profession, recent graduation, or your enthusiasm and passion for your field.

Unique traits: Mention specific qualities and skills that set each individual apart. For example, your flair for creativity in graphic design, dedication to sustainable design in engineering, or compassion and commitment to patient care in health care.

Interests and hobbies: Provide a glimpse into your interests and hobbies outside of your professional pursuits. For example, mention that you enjoy exploring new art forms, are passionate about college basketball, or that you volunteer at community health fairs.

Seeking a mentor: Mention that you're actively seeking a mentor in relevant fields. It specifies the type of mentor you are looking for and the areas in which you hope a mentor can support you.

Career goals: Outline your aspirations and long-term career goals, such as building a design portfolio, working on sustainable projects and becoming a leader in sustainable design, or excelling in nursing practice and pursuing health care leadership roles.

What Not to Include

Avoid the following in your introduction:

Illicit language: Crude language can be divisive, as people have different sensitivities to it. It's best to steer clear of any crude language, suggestive innuendos, references to drugs or alcohol, or explicit content. Remember, your potential mentor might have a different perspective, and it's not considered professional in most environments. Instead, showcase your personality through other means.

False information: Trust is essential when building relationships. Avoid providing false details about your role, career, or any other aspect. Being dishonest is not only poor professional etiquette but also detrimental to creating meaningful connections.

Salary information: Salary information is not relevant to the initial conversation. While discussing salaries with friends to support each other's career growth is beneficial, it's best to avoid mentioning your salary when introducing yourself to strangers. Save these discussions for situations where it's appropriate, such as negotiations with human resources or when discussing your career progress with your mentor.

Negative details about your current situation: How you talk about others can shape how people perceive you. Even if your current work situation is challenging, avoid bringing up negative details in your first introduction. Aim to promote a growth mindset rather than sharing gossip. Negative comments about company culture, bosses, coworkers, or yourself should be avoided when introducing yourself to potential mentors.

Example 1: Sabrine the Engineer

30-Second Elevator Overview

I'm a mechanical engineer with a genuine passion for innovation. Though I've recently entered the professional engineering world, I bring a fresh perspective and a strong technical background to solving complex challenges in sustainable design and renewable energy. I'm dedicated to developing solutions that have a meaningful impact on both society and the environment.

In my free time, you'll often find me on the basketball court, feeding my competitive spirit. Currently, I'm in search of a mentor, ideally an experienced engineer or engineering manager, who can share insights into sustainable design practices and help guide my professional development. I'm eager to dive into more significant engineering projects, specifically here in New York; it's just such a big city and hard to meet people.

15-Second Elevator Overview

I'm a mechanical engineer focused on innovation and sustainable design. There's something immensely satisfying about unraveling complex challenges and sculpting them into sustainable solutions. My ultimate aim is to join projects that leave a significant mark on the city, and I'm starting to meet others who have already done the same.

Double Opt-In Overview

Sabrine, a newly minted mechanical engineer, possesses a keen interest in innovation. With her solid technical foundation and aptitude for problem solving, she consistently approaches engineering challenges with creativity and determination. Her commitment to sustainable design and renewable energy pushes her to devise solutions that are both environmentally conscious and socially influential. Beyond the lab, Sabrine is an avid basketball enthusiast and enjoys learning more about the city. She's currently on the lookout for a seasoned engineering mentor to provide guidance in the industry, share expertise in sustainable design, and aid in her professional development. With the right mentorship, Sabrine is poised to spearhead significant engineering projects and make meaningful strides in mechanical engineering.

Example 2: Tiffany the Brand Manager

30-Second Elevator Overview

I'm a brand manager at [company name], with a focus on brand storytelling. My six years in marketing have shaped my ability to weave together stories that not only engage our audience but also resonate with their core values and giving our clients data to prove it's working.

At this point in my career, I'm actively seeking a mentor with a rich background in marketing leadership or entrepreneurship. I envision myself taking the reins on prominent marketing campaigns, contributing to the success of major brands, and ultimately, launching my own marketing agency.

15-Second Overview

As a brand manager, crafting compelling campaigns that resonate with audiences is what I thrive on. I'm here to meet other marketing professionals and excited to connect with people that have been in the industry for years or have their own agency, as that's a goal of mine in the future and I'm curious how it's done.

Double Opt-In

In her role as a brand manager at [company name], Tiffany brings a strategic and analytical approach to brand storytelling and campaign development, always leveraging data to drive decision-making and optimize marketing efforts. With a clear vision of her career trajectory in the marketing sphere, Tiffany is not just committed to her professional growth; she's also keen to engage in the joy of competition, be it beating her twin sister at pickleball or perfecting the family banana bread recipe.

Tiffany is currently on the lookout for a mentor with a wealth of experience in marketing leadership or entrepreneurship within the marketing industry. She's eager to deepen her understanding of effective strategy development across various industries, sharpen her leadership skills, and expand her professional network. Ultimately, Tiffany envisions herself starting her own marketing agency, leading high-impact campaigns for top-tier brands. She knows that the right mentor will be instrumental in helping her realize this vision.

Example 3: Sarah the Nurse

30-Second Elevator Overview

I just graduated from nursing school, and I'm excited to start making a difference in people's lives as a health care professional. I've seen friends and family go through tough times health-wise, and it made me want to be there for patients when they need it most.

Outside of the hospital, I love hitting the river for some kayaking, and, of course, cheering on the University of Texas at Austin in any sport I can. Hook 'em Horns!

Right now, I'm looking for a mentor with experience in nursing or health care administration to help me fine-tune my clinical skills and really get the hang of how health care systems work. I've got some big career goals in nursing, and I'm hoping to find a mentor who can guide me in the right direction to achieve them.

15-Second Elevator Overview

Comforting patients in their time of need and collaborating with the brightest minds in the medical field fueled my desire to become a nurse. Having recently graduated, I'm diving into different groups and events in search of my tribe and a mentor to guide my first steps in my career.

Double Opt-In

Sarah Thompson is a compassionate aspiring nurse committed to patient care. Fresh out of nursing school, she is ready to start her journey in the health care world, seeking to make a positive impact on people's lives. Whether it's providing comfort to patients or working alongside medical teams to offer comprehensive care, she brings empathy and responsibility to her role. Away from hospital duties, you'll find Sarah volunteering at community health fairs, advocating for wellness, and encouraging healthy lifestyles. She is on the lookout for a mentor with a background in nursing or health care administration who can assist her in honing her clinical skills, understanding the intricacies of health care systems, and guiding her toward her long-term career aspirations in nursing. With the support of a mentor, she aspires to excel in her practice, pursue specialized training in health care administration leadership, and contribute to improving health care outcomes in her community.

Exercise to Craft Your Own: Step-by-Step Guide to Writing a Short Overview

Use this template as a starting point to craft your short overview. Customize it to reflect your unique experiences, goals, and aspirations. Keep it concise, friendly, and professional. Once you have completed the exercise, review it to ensure it effectively represents you and your aspirations. Try practicing with friends and family to see which versions sound the most like you—just with a little more professional polish.

1. Introduction: Start by introducing yourself with your full name and your profession or recent accomplishment. For example, "I am [full name], a [your profession/recent accomplishment]."

2. Highlight your passion: Mention your enthusiasm and passion for your chosen field. Use descriptive words to showcase your genuine interest. For example, "I am deeply passionate about [your field] and am eager to make a mark in the world of [your industry]."

3. Unique qualities: Highlight what makes you unique and stand out in your field. This can include your fresh perspective, creative approach, or any other special skills you possess. For example, "I bring a fresh perspective given my transition from defense contracting to management consulting, and a flair for creativity. I bring a unique touch to every project I take on."

4. Professional achievements: Briefly mention some of your notable achievements or experiences in your field. Focus on the projects you have worked on or any accomplishments that showcase your skills. For example, "I just finished a project for a $55M client, where I was responsible for researching the client's competitors. We ended up finding a new way to take over the market because of that, so I'm excited I got to be on that team."

5. Seeking a mentor: Clearly state that you are actively seeking a mentor and specify the type of mentor you are looking for. For example, "I am actively seeking a mentor who is an established graphic designer or creative director, someone who can guide me in refining my photo-editing skills, understanding client needs, and navigating the competitive design industry."

6. Mentorship goals: Describe the goals you hope to achieve with the help of a mentor. Be specific about the areas in which you want to grow and develop. For example, "With the guidance of a mentor, my goal is to build a strong design portfolio, secure exciting projects with renowned brands, and eventually establish my own design studio."

⬛ ⬛ ⬛

Crafting a succinct and compelling elevator overview is a pivotal step in presenting yourself to prospective mentors and building a meaningful mentor-mentee relationship. As you reflect on your unique skills and experiences, remember to infuse your personality into your narrative. This personal touch transforms a simple list of facts into a story that resonates and connects with others. With a well-prepared elevator overview, you'll be poised to engage with potential mentors confidently, knowing that you are showcasing the best version of yourself. And don't forget, this handy overview also serves as an excellent response to the classic job interview question "Tell us about yourself."

Armed with your elevator overview, you're ready to navigate the mentorship landscape and make lasting connections that will support and enrich your professional journey. In the next chapter, we will explore the strategies for conducting meetings with your potential mentors, following your initial brief conversations. You will receive the necessary information to maintain organization and foster authentic relationships throughout the process.

6

Genuine Connections: Conducting Meetings with Future Mentors

HAVING THE FIRST initial conversations with a potential mentor can be an intimidating part of the process. There can be nerves, excitement, and questions. Because those feelings are natural and a realistic response to meeting someone new, help alleviate undue pressure by feeling confident about the conversation before you even have it.

An important note: I suggest refraining from directly expressing your intent to find a mentor during the early stages of your interactions. Jumping into the mentorship discussion too hastily can create unnecessary pressure and potentially hinder the relationship's natural development. Rather than put this question at the forefront of your conversations, focus on building a genuine connection and understanding each other better. It's more beneficial to take your time, learn from one another, and allow the mentorship journey to unfold organically.

Now that you've identified potential mentors and reached out to them, the next step is to conduct introductory meetings to see whether there's a good fit. It's an opportunity to connect on a personal level, understand each other's goals, and determine whether there's a potential mentor-mentee fit. This phase is not about formalities or impressing them with your accomplishments. I was guilty of trying to

It's about being genuine, engaging in meaningful conversation, and evaluating whether you and the other person have the chemistry that is so important for a mentorship journey together.

fit in every possible accomplishment and detail when I first started meeting mentors, and while they were gracious, there was room for improvement. Instead, it's about being genuine, engaging in meaningful conversation, and evaluating whether you and the other person have the chemistry that is so important for a mentorship journey together. Think of it as a conversation with a potential collaborator, guide, and source of inspiration.

Approaching these meetings with the right mindset is essential. You're not being interviewed for a job; it's an opportunity to explore and see whether this mentor aligns with your goals and values. In this section, we'll go into strategies to keep these first meetings casual, engaging, and productive. By following these guidelines, you can create a meaningful connection that can lead to a fruitful mentorship.

These early interactions should revolve around your genuine interest in their background, experiences, and insights. As your mentorship journey progresses, the right time for discussing mentorship dynamics will naturally present itself.

Organizing Your Mentor Network

You may be considering anywhere from 1 to 10 people as mentors, and that can be a lot to manage. It's critical to have a focused strategy. With an emphasis on *quality over quantity*, you allow for meaningful, substantive conversations, leading to swifter progress. Start with a list of 10 potential mentors who resonate with your goals and initiate relationships with intention and purpose.

I highly recommend creating a mentor tracker as an invaluable resource to support your mentorship journey. This tool is designed to help you streamline and simplify the process of managing your potential mentors. Whether you're meeting mentors in person or through virtual channels, the mentor tracker will be your ally in staying organized and making well-informed decisions that benefit your mentorship relationships.

The mentor tracker serves as your personalized mentor management system. It's a simple yet effective way to keep essential information about your potential mentors organized and easily accessible. This tool is particularly useful for tracking various details, including contact information, meeting schedules, key takeaways from your conversations, and follow-up actions. By centralizing all this information in one place, you'll find it much easier to engage with your mentors effectively and establish meaningful connections.

Making Your Mentor Tracker

Create your columns (from left column to right):

- Name
- Company
- Position
- LinkedIn profile URL
- When/where you met: location, event, mutual connection
- Mutual connection: if you have any mutual connections either on LinkedIn or in your social communities, list those here
- Area of focus: their key area of focus; this can be a skill, industry, or role.
- Goal they support: have your top three goals, and list what goal the mentor prospect supports; if they don't support one of your top three goals, leave that box blank.
- Key questions: this is where you list the questions you want to ask the mentor prospect during your conversation; having these prepared in advance allows you to get out of your head and focus on the conversation taking place, trusting if you feel stuck or the conversation slows, you have backup questions ready to support you.
- Stage: this is where you list where you are in learning about your mentor; create the following options:
  - First introduction
  - First meeting scheduled
  - Second/third meeting scheduled

      o Not moving forward

      o Making the ask

Having these prepared in advance will help you update your tracker faster and know which people you need to follow up with next.

■ Notes: any next steps, advice given during the conversation, or general notes you want to take about the conversation.

How to Use Your Mentor Tracker

1. Add the names and information of potential mentors to the spreadsheet.

2. Develop questions to ask in your first meeting with a potential mentor based on what you're working on and their career. You can refer back to the question examples for the different types of mentors in Chapter 3.

3. Update the "Stage" column after interactions with your potential mentors or as you meet new people.

4. The "Notes" section is used to take down anything the potential mentor mentions during your meetings that you want to refer back to. This can include a book recommendation, their response to your current work situation, their dog's name, whatever you want to make sure you remember for your follow-up conversations. This section may be needed depending on how many potential mentors you're speaking with.

Send a Calendar Invitation

Once you've received confirmation of the mentor's date and time that they're available for the meeting, take the next step by sending your potential mentor a well-structured calendar invitation. This should include essential details such as the meeting date, start and end times, chosen meeting platform or location, and a link to your LinkedIn profile. When planning a virtual meeting, aim for a 30-minute conversation, while in-person meetings can extend to 45–50 minutes. This seemingly minor step reflects your professionalism and consideration for your and your mentor's time. Additionally, sending a calendar invitation ensures that both parties remain well prepared and reminded as the meeting approaches.

Keep It Professional and Relaxed

When approaching an introductory meeting with a potential mentor, remember that the goal is to foster an authentic connection. You want them to know who you are professionally, and you want to know who they are too. You want to strike a balance of showing you've done your homework on them, while also leaving plenty of room for them to share more about themselves. Keep the atmosphere casual and relaxed. The meeting is a chance to get to know the person, rather than a formal interview. This not only eases any tension but also creates a more open and comfortable environment for both parties.

Approach the meeting as a chance to know the person behind the professional title. Think about how you'd want to be treated during a first conversation with someone. Approach the meeting with a friendly and open demeanor. A genuine interest in getting to know them will go a long way in setting the right tone. The more comfortable and authentic you are, the easier it will be to build rapport with your potential mentor. Mentors are people too, and they appreciate genuine interactions. Begin with a light icebreaker—it could be as simple as discussing a recent industry event, sharing a common interest, or even commenting on the weather. By setting a casual tone, you create a space where both parties can engage openly and authentically.

> *The more comfortable and authentic you are, the easier it will be to build rapport with your potential mentor. Mentors are people too, and they appreciate genuine interactions.*

Take the Pressure Off: Exploring without Commitment

Enter the introductory meeting with the mindset that you're exploring possibilities, not making a binding decision. It's natural to feel a sense of anticipation before meeting a potential mentor, but it's important to ease the pressure you may be placing on yourself. Approach the meeting with the mindset of exploration rather than a high-stakes decision. This is your chance to learn more about the mentor's experiences, insights, and values. Similarly, the mentor is also gauging if there's a genuine connection and alignment of goals. Embracing the idea that this is a mutual exploration allows for a more relaxed and authentic exchange.

Learn More about Them: Ask Conversational Questions

Engage your potential mentor in a conversation by asking open-ended and conversational questions. Ask about their own mentors and how those relationships influenced their success. Show a genuine interest in their work and the lessons they've learned along the way.

Prepare a list of conversational questions that allow you to uncover details of their journey. Inquire about their career milestones, challenges they've overcome, and lessons they've learned along the way. Ask about their sources of inspiration, favorite books, or hobbies. These questions not only provide valuable insights but also showcase your genuine interest in their experiences.

Questions can include:

- "I noticed you made the switch from working as a manager at a tech company to working as a director at a global clothing brand. What was the experience of shifting industries like for you? Did you notice a big shift in responsibilities from manager to director?"
- "I'm struggling to find the balance between creating monthly goals that will help with my case for a promotion, while also improving my resume and likelihood of attracting attention from recruiters at different companies. How have you found that balance when job searching?"
- "What are recommendations for shortening sales cycles? Could you speak on best practices for leadership structures to have the most effective coverage across potential customers?"
- "I'm returning to work after four years of focusing on my family. You mentioned in a podcast interview that you had a similar

time frame where you did the same. What were the first steps you took to feel mentally and emotionally ready to return to work?"

- "I'm new to the city and want to explore some fun things to do when I need a break and want to meet new people. You mentioned hiking in your LinkedIn post yesterday. What are some good trails nearby that you'd recommend?"
- "How do you enjoy serving on the board of [nonprofit name]. I'm interested in expanding my network to connect with a broader group of people, as I think about my future career goals. Do you recommend volunteering or joining a board to support that?"

This approach not only makes the conversation more enjoyable but also helps you gain valuable insights into their mentoring style.

Be Open to the Natural Flow

While it's important to have a few questions in mind, avoid rehearsed scripts or overthinking every word, and be open to the natural flow of the conversation. Sometimes, the most valuable insights and connections come from unexpected areas of discussion. Write your questions down in a notebook ahead of the meeting so you can be present during the conversation. If you get to them, great. If not and the conversation was valuable, that's great too and you can set up a second meeting as needed. If the mentor shares personal stories or anecdotes, be an active listener. Engage with their experiences and demonstrate your receptiveness to their guidance. Being flexible and adaptable during the meeting shows that you're genuinely interested in building a meaningful relationship.

Mentorship is a two-way street, and the introductory meeting is a chance to assess if your personalities and aspirations align. Be prepared to share your own career aspirations and challenges as well. Allow the conversation to veer into unexpected topics—you may discover shared values, interests, or even new perspectives that enhance the mentorship dynamic.

> *Mentorship is a two-way street, and the introductory meeting is a chance to assess if your personalities and aspirations align.*

Manage Your Meeting Time

During engaging conversations, it's easy for time to slip by unnoticed. Engaging discussions can often create a time distortion, making a 45-minute conversation feel as if it's only been 20 minutes. However, respecting both your and your potential mentor's time is key. To ensure efficient conversations, consider using a timer. If you're meeting virtually for 30 minutes, set it to alert you when five to seven minutes remain. For in-person meetings lasting 45–50 minutes, set the timer to notify you when you have around 10 minutes left. This gentle reminder allows you to gracefully transition into wrapping up the conversation. Politely inform your potential mentor that you're using a timer to help manage the time effectively.

Important: once your timer is set, keep your phone out of sight and have notifications turned off. By minimizing distractions, you maintain the natural flow of conversation without interruptions.

Ending the Meeting

When it comes to making a positive impression, how you end a meeting is as much of an impression-making moment as when you start it. When your timer alerts you that you have about 10 minutes left in the in-person conversation, take the opportunity to let your conversation partner know that you're entering the final stretch of your discussion. Something simple such as "That's my timer letting us know we have about 10 minutes before our meeting time frame is over. I want to make sure I don't hold you for too long, although I am enjoying this conversation" will do. Express your enjoyment of the discussion and highlight a particular point they made.

Then, consider asking, "Is there anything I can assist you with?" This question is a standard part of my interactions with mentors and new acquaintances. It's sincere; I genuinely want to offer help where I can. Simultaneously, it signifies that you're interested in fostering a two-way relationship in a highly transactional world, a real differentiator. Mentorship thrives on collaboration. By asking an open-ended question like this, you give your mentor the chance to share areas where they might welcome support. This approach sets you apart from others seeking their time. Make it a practice to jot down any assistance they might require. This not only showcases your proactive attitude but also ensures that you follow up on their needs effectively. Make sure to follow up if there are areas where you can support them.

Leave Space for Reflection in Your Decision-Making

Imagine two people purchasing a new outfit for an upcoming event. Person 1 rushes into a decision, driven by a sense of urgency without considering outside details. They quickly make a choice without carefully considering the details of the purchase, leading to regrets later on when they realize it wasn't what they truly needed. On the other hand, person 2 plans ahead, taking into account the complete ensemble. They focus on how the outfit fits and how comfortable they feel wearing it and approach the decision with a mindset geared toward enjoying the entire event in something they can wear more than once. This careful consideration increases the likelihood of their satisfaction with the outfit and their choice, increasing their confidence in their decision-making skills.

It goes without saying that mentors and outfits are vastly different topics, but the decision-making mindset you bring to selecting mentors is coming from the same place. If you tend to approach decision-making hastily or with a scarcity mindset, there's a high likelihood of that same mentality entering your mentor decision-making. It might feel as though there's a need for an immediate decision, similar to person 1's rushed purchase. Just as person 2 benefits from thoughtful consideration, take the time you need to reflect and ensure a mentorship relationship aligns with your goals and aspirations.

If you tend to approach decision-making hastily or with a scarcity mindset, there's a high likelihood of that same mentality entering your mentor decision-making.

Send a Thank-You Note

The simple act of saying, "Thank you" holds remarkable power. With our busy lives, it's often easy to overlook the importance of taking a brief moment to convey appreciation for someone's time and insights.

Regardless of whether you intend to move forward or not, sending a quick and thoughtful note of gratitude via your ongoing communication method can make a positive impact. Share something specific you learned during your conversation. If there were any follow-up items or action points discussed, provide a clear timeline for your intended follow-up. Keep the message concise, professional, and personalized. For example, if they shared being new to your city and you reside there too, you could include a short list of local activities, showcasing your attentive and helpful nature.

Below Is a Thank-You Note Template to Get You Started:

Email subject line: Thank you
Hi [name],

I wanted to take a moment to thank you for your time [yesterday, this morning, this afternoon—somewhere within a 24-hour time frame]. Your insights and perspectives have left a lasting impression.

One key takeaway for me was [mention a specific point that resonated with you in one sentence]. Your perspective opened my eyes, and I'm already brainstorming ways to apply it to my [life, journey, next meeting, next project, something specific but no more than five words].

I appreciate your willingness to share your experiences and knowledge. It's clear that your expertise will be instrumental in helping me navigate the path ahead. I'm looking forward to the possibility of continuing our conversation.

Thanks again for sharing your story and your time. Please let me know if there's anything I can do to be helpful with your goals as well.

Best regards,
[Your first name]

☐ ☒ ☒

[Your first and last name,
link to your LinkedIn profile,
your personal website or portfolio if it's relevant]

Evaluating Compatibility

After the introductory meeting, take time to assess whether there's a sense of compatibility. Reflect on whether the conversation felt natural, if their insights resonated with you, and if you can envision a potential mentor-mentee relationship. Refer back to the mentor tracking spreadsheet you created earlier in this chapter. Consider if the mentor's experiences, values, and approach align with your goals and aspirations. Did you feel a genuine connection? Did the conversation leave you inspired and motivated? If the answer is yes, it may be worth exploring the possibility of a mentorship relationship further.

Reach out with a follow-up message expressing your interest in continuing the conversation and seeking their guidance. In this outreach, express your gratitude for the meeting and reiterate your interest in the possibility of mentorship. Gauge their response to see whether they are open to further discussions.

If both you and the mentor feel there's potential for a mentoring relationship, take the next step and schedule a follow-up meeting. This could be a more in-depth discussion about your goals and how the mentor can guide you in achieving them.

What to Avoid during Your Conversations

When having meetings with potential mentors, it's important to approach the interaction with professionalism and mutual respect. To ensure a productive and positive experience, here are some things to avoid:

Being unprepared: Avoid going into the meeting without doing your homework. Research the mentor's background, accomplishments, and areas of expertise so you can engage in a meaningful conversation. Avoid attending the meeting without a clear agenda or specific questions. If you're meeting in person, bring a notebook and pen. If you're meeting virtually, have a method to take notes during your conversation that will not be distracting. Do not use your phone as your note-taking tool of choice in either scenario.

Monopolizing the conversation: This can happen when you're feeling nervous and want to make sure you hit every possible achievement during the conversation. Avoid dominating the conversation with your own agenda or talking only about yourself. Remember to listen actively and show genuine interest in the mentor's insights and experiences.

Focusing solely on personal gain: Don't make the conversation solely about what the mentor can do for you. Leave space to take interest in their experiences and offer value in return. Don't treat the mentorship as a transaction. Focus on building a genuine connection rather than solely seeking short-term benefits.

Overwhelming your potential mentor with questions: While questions are important, avoid bombarding the mentor with an excessive number of questions that do not leave room for an engaging dialogue about their response. Prioritize your questions and give them time to provide thoughtful responses.

Failing to follow up: After the meeting, avoid neglecting to follow up with a thank-you note or an update on your progress. Express your gratitude and share any action steps you've taken based on their advice.

Pressuring for immediate commitment: Avoid pressuring the mentor to commit to a long-term mentoring relationship during the initial meeting. Give both parties time to assess compatibility.

Overstepping boundaries: Avoid asking overly personal or intrusive questions. Avoid oversharing personal or sensitive information unless it's relevant to the mentorship. Maintain a professional demeanor and respect their privacy.

Criticizing or complaining: Avoid negative discussions about your current situation, job, or industry. Keep the conversation positive and forward-focused.

Lacking professionalism: Steer clear of using overly casual language, slang, or inappropriate humor. Maintain a professional tone throughout the meeting.

Being impatient: Avoid rushing the process or expecting immediate results. Building a mentorship relationship takes time, and it's important to nurture the connection over time.

Lacking clear objectives: Avoid entering the meeting without a clear idea of what you hope to achieve from the mentorship. Have specific goals and objectives in mind to guide the conversation.

Neglecting to listen: Avoid focusing solely on what you want to say. Listen actively to the mentor's guidance and ask follow-up questions to deepen your understanding.

By remembering and avoiding these common pitfalls, you can approach meetings with potential mentors in a respectful, considerate, and productive manner that enhances your chances of forming valuable mentorship relationships.

Conducting introductory meetings with potential mentors is an exciting and rewarding process. By keeping the conversation casual, engaging, and free of pressure, you create an environment where both you and the mentor can authentically connect. This is an exploration phase, and the goal is to determine whether there's a natural fit for a mentoring relationship. Be open, curious, and genuine in your interactions, and the right mentor will naturally emerge to support you on your career journey.

After meeting with potential mentors and determining whether they are well-suited to your objectives, the next step is to gauge their interest in proceeding. This involves inviting them to become your mentor. The following chapter will guide you in crafting a compelling, genuine proposal based on your discussions with the mentor, as well as outlining subsequent actions for your mentoring relationship.

7

The Invitation: Asking Someone
to Be Your Mentor

ONCE YOU'VE IDENTIFIED the person who is a good fit for you and your goals, it's time for the delicate task of asking them to be your mentor. When it comes to structuring the ask, there are certain phrases and approaches that can make all the difference. It can be nerve-wracking and feel daunting, but don't worry. From knowing the right moment to ask to overcoming any self-doubt or fear, this chapter will help you enter those conversations feeling genuine, clear, and purposeful. This chapter will empower you to establish a meaningful mentorship relationship that fosters growth and learning for both parties involved.

> Note: Not everyone will need to go through the process of officially asking someone to be their mentor. If you have a preexisting relationship that has evolved into a mentee-mentor relationship organically, or you feel you're on the same page, that's amazing. Continue reading with Chapter 8. Everyone else, let's continue with this chapter to unpack how to frame your ask to a mentor and ensure you're set up for success.

We'll cover the best practices for framing your request in a way that's respectful, professional, and genuine. We'll explore why it's important to approach your potential mentor as a human first and not as a means to an end.

It's important to set goals and establish a timeline for your working relationship. We'll discuss how to work with your mentor to identify your objectives and map out a path to achieving them. Finally, we'll outline the different phases of a mentor relationship, from the early stages of getting to know one another to a longer-term mentor-mentee relationship that can help drive your career growth forward.

> *Yet it's not just about identifying the right person—it's about approaching them in a way that resonates with their values and aligns with your aspirations.*

Finding a mentor is a pivotal step in your professional growth and development. Yet it's not just about identifying the right person—it's about approaching them in a way that resonates with their values and aligns with your aspirations.

Oftentimes making the ask is the hardest part of moving forward in the process. I am always slightly nervous when it comes to this part of the process. When making the ask to invite someone to be a mentor on your journey, there's a short conversation to have with them using the components I outline here. I used this for all of my early discussions with my own mentors. This template makes it easier to walk the potential mentor through your headspace, intentions, and objectives. The clearer you can make the ask, the easier it is for the mentor to confirm whether they are in a position to join you and proceed with the next steps or whether they're not a fit at this time.

The *ask template* is another exercise included at the end of the chapter on asking someone to be your mentor. It is a fill-in-the-blank template you can use when crafting your ask to a potential mentor. The template includes prompts such as "I am reaching out to you because . . ." and "My goals for this mentorship are . . ." This exercise is designed to help you structure your ask in a professional yet personable way and ensure you're making a clear and compelling case for why this person should be your mentor.

Starting the Conversation: Your Invitation Email

Before drafting your mentorship invitation, take a moment to reflect on why you're drawn to this specific individual as a potential mentor. Mentorship is not solely about gaining or refining skills; it's about building a connection with someone who resonates with your aspirations and values. This is the perfect time to go to your mentor tracker spreadsheet. It may be helpful to review any notes that you took over your previous conversations and update it with any new information you've learned. Start by reflecting on what specifically draws you to them—is it their career trajectory, their values, their expertise, or their accomplishments? Think about common interests, experiences, or viewpoints that create a genuine human connection.

Once you've processed this information, it's time to compose an email inviting the potential mentor to discuss the prospect of working together. Craft your email to maintain a professional, concise, and clear tone, focusing on setting up a meeting rather than directly requesting mentorship.

Here Is an Outreach Template to Use When Asking to Schedule Your Conversation

Hello [name],

[Greeting such as "I hope you had a great weekend," "How was your son's birthday party?" or "How is your week going so far?"]. I've genuinely enjoyed our conversations and the insights into your career. As you're aware, I've been actively seeking a mentor with your impressive skill set, specifically [one to three focus areas here; one short sentence or phrase each]. I'm interested in the prospect of exploring potential collaboration further and sharing my vision for a collective effort. Could we schedule a conversation in the upcoming weeks to discuss this in more detail? Your input would be invaluable. If you're interested, please let me know your availability, and I'll send a calendar invitation.

Thank you for considering this, and I'm looking forward to the possibility of connecting.

Best regards,

[Your name]

How to Structure Your Mentor Invitation Meeting

If the person you reach out to is interested in continuing the conversation, use the following outline to conduct an organized and collaborative meeting with them. The goal of this meeting is to confirm whether they're available and interested in serving as your mentor, align on your initial goals, and confirm their bandwidth to join you on your journey.

Explain Why You Want Them as a Mentor

Mentors are more likely to invest their time and knowledge in someone who appreciates their unique qualities. Personalize your approach to show that you've done your homework and genuinely admire what they bring to the table.

The foundation of any successful mentorship relationship lies in the authenticity of your connection with your potential mentor. Mentors are more likely to invest their time and knowledge in someone who appreciates their unique qualities. Personalize your approach to show that you've done your homework and genuinely admire what they bring to the table.

Begin your request by expressing your genuine admiration for their achievements, expertise, and the impact they've made in their field. Highlight specific qualities or accomplishments that resonate with you. This personal touch demonstrates that your interest is rooted in a deep appreciation for their contributions, setting the stage for a meaningful mentorship journey. Clearly list the skills or strengths they possess that you want to focus on within your career. Keep it to one to three brief bullets when writing down your talking points.

Clearly Define Your Goals

Your mentorship invitation should clearly outline your goals and what you aspire to achieve through the guidance of your potential mentor. Clearly articulate what you hope to achieve through mentorship *with them specifically*. Whether it's acquiring new skills, gaining industry insights, or refining your career goals, your potential mentor should understand what's in it for them as well. Clarifying your objectives not only demonstrates your commitment but also helps potential mentors understand how they can contribute effectively to your growth. Share how achieving these goals aligns with your overall career trajectory and long-term ambitions.

Template:

Throughout my career, I've aspired to [describe your career goals or aspirations], and your journey resonates deeply with my own path. Your ability to [mention a relevant skill or accomplishment] aligns perfectly with my pursuit of [your goal]. I believe that learning from your experiences would help me grow and bring me closer to achieving [your career objective].

Example 1:

Throughout my career, I've aspired to increase my public speaking opportunities to solidify my positioning as a leader in people operations, and your journey resonates deeply with my own path. Your ability to present on panels and keynotes on how leaders can improve their team culture through sustainable people operations practices aligns perfectly with my pursuit of becoming a director in this field in the next two years. I believe that learning from your experiences would help me grow and bring me closer to achieving the skill sets required for this promotion and speaking opportunities.

Example 2:

Throughout my career, I've aspired to create a brand that not only crafts exquisite jewelry but also resonates with the stories and lives of its wearers, and your journey resonates deeply with my own path. Your ability to blend innovative design with sustainable practices aligns perfectly with my pursuit of establishing a jewelry line that celebrates both beauty and ethics. I believe that learning from your experiences would help me grow and bring me closer to achieving my career objective of being a pioneering force in the eco-conscious luxury market.

Time Requirement: Defining the Commitment

The biggest consideration for mentors entering into a mentor relationship is time. This is especially true for women who consider becoming mentors—75% say the time commitment is their biggest concern, with subject matter expertise (54%), and their relation to the mentee (also 54%) the second and third concerns, respectively.[1] With time constraints being such a big factor, it is important to emphasize the time commitment up front to ensure you're on the same page.

In your conversation, be transparent about the time commitment you're seeking from them. It's helpful to propose a realistic frequency of interactions, whether it's a monthly meeting, biweekly check-ins, or occasional coffee chats. Emphasize your commitment to valuing their time and that you are open to their suggestions for structuring the mentorship schedule. Setting clear expectations up front helps both you and your mentor manage time effectively.

Be prepared to accommodate their availability. Showing consideration for their schedule demonstrates your professionalism and commitment to making the mentorship valuable for both parties.

Example:

Recognizing the value of your time, I wanted to start with [mention the frequency and duration of interactions] first and adjust, depending on how we both feel. I'm committed to making our interactions efficient, engaging, and mutually beneficial. I want to respect your schedule.

Pause 1: Confirm Their Interest in Mentorship

Conversations are most fruitful when they're two-way streets. Take a moment to seek feedback from your potential mentor regarding the information you've provided. This proactive step not only ensures you're investing your time effectively but also allows you to confirm their interest in moving forward before going into an extensive dialogue. Gauge their curiosity and availability for mentorship based on the details you've shared earlier. If they express interest in further exploration, proceed with the following steps.

Outline of Growth Phases: Charting Your Mentorship Path

Provide a structured plan of how you envision the mentorship unfolding. Consider a timeline, for example one to two months, with clear phases that outline the steps you intend to take. Detail the key milestones, objectives, and activities you intend to accomplish during each phase. Your outline provides a clear road map that guides the mentorship toward achieving concrete outcomes.

Example:

> Break down the mentorship into manageable milestones. For
> example, if your goal involves enhancing your presentation skills,
> your phases might include researching effective techniques, prac-
> ticing in low-pressure settings, and eventually delivering a pres-
> entation to a small group. Presenting your plan in phases not only
> showcases your dedication but also provides your potential
> mentor with a tangible road map of what to expect.

Pause 2: Get Feedback on Your Approach

With their expressed interest in mentoring, the next step is to ensure
alignment regarding the specifics of your collaboration. This initial
alignment lays the foundation for the frequency and nature of your
interactions, confirming whether their expertise aligns with your needs
and objectives. It also initiates the learning process, benefiting from
their experience to fine-tune your approach. By seeking feedback and
clarifying expectations, you can optimize your mentorship engagement
and create a strong starting point for your partnership.

Example:

> *Pick one of the following to ask your mentor:*
>
> - *Is this how you would approach this?*
> - *Is there anything missing from what I shared?*
> - *Is there a more streamlined approach you recommend?*

Handling If They Say No

If a potential mentor declines your invitation, it's important to handle
the situation with composure and professionalism. Here's how you can
navigate this situation:

> **Do not take it personally:** This is not a reflection of you, your
> career trajectory, or your ability to be mentored.

Express understanding: Thank them for taking the time to consider your request, and express your understanding of their decision.

Stay positive: Maintain a positive and gracious tone in your response. Avoid sounding disappointed or discouraged, as this is a natural part of the mentorship process.

Seek feedback: Politely ask for feedback on their decision. This can provide valuable insights into their reasons and help you improve your approach in the future.

Keep the door open: Express your openness to any future opportunities for collaboration, networking, or even occasional advice. This shows your professionalism and willingness to maintain a positive connection.

Thank them again: Conclude your response by thanking them once more for their time and consideration. This leaves a positive impression and ensures the door is left open for potential interactions down the road.

Example Response:

Hi [name],

Thank you for considering my request and taking the time to discuss the possibility of mentorship. While I understand and respect your decision, I wanted to express my gratitude for your willingness to consider the mentorship opportunity. Your insights and expertise are inspiring, and I hope our paths may cross in the future.

Thank you again for your time, and I look forward to staying connected. Wishing you continued success in all your endeavors.

Best regards,

[Your name]

Your Mentor Is Not Your Employee; I Repeat: Your Mentor Is Not Your Employee

Remember, this meeting isn't about creating a to-do list for your potential mentor. It's an opportunity for interactive dialogue where you seek their valuable input. Discuss their availability, preferred means of communication, and ensure alignment. Keep the tone positive, keep it concise, and inquire about their suggested next steps. As you conclude the meeting, convey your enthusiasm in a professional manner and indicate when you plan to follow up.

⬛ ⬛ ⬛

Asking someone to be your mentor is a significant step that requires thoughtfulness and clarity. By emphasizing your genuine appreciation, outlining your goals, discussing the time commitment, and providing a structured plan, you're setting the stage for a productive and mutually rewarding mentorship. Remember, being human, respectful, and proactive in your approach will greatly increase the likelihood of receiving a positive response. Your request should resonate with sincerity, reflecting your commitment to growth and your potential mentor's role in your professional journey.

Securing a new mentor marks just the beginning of your mentoring relationship. In the next chapter, we'll focus on fostering a lasting relationship with your mentor starting with your first official meeting. We'll cover strategies for collaborating effectively to ensure a mutually beneficial and enriching experience for everyone involved.

8

Preparing for Mentor Interactions for Better Results

CONGRATULATIONS! BY FOLLOWING the process, investing effort, broad-ening your network, and bravely inviting someone to accompany you on your career path as a mentor, you've successfully found a mentor to support your professional growth. That took dedication, and now you're ready to build a relationship with this mentor. It can be easy to focus solely on the mentor search and romanticize the process that you just went through, without realizing that the real work comes in building the relationship and working together once you've decided to work together. It's now time to cultivate a mentorship relationship that thrives on open communication, mutual respect, and shared learning.

> Note: While mentorship is a valuable relationship, an effective approach to expanding on your mentorship sessions is to learn from diverse sources. Avoid solely relying on your mentor for all your professional development needs. Explore various learning avenues, including books, webinars, and networking events, to broaden your knowledge and perspectives.

It's natural to have some anxiety about how to manage the relationship. Common questions about maintaining a mentor relationship are:

- How do I conduct meetings with my mentors? What do I do during these meetings?
- I'm nervous. What do I do as my first step?
- What do I work on with a mentor?
- How much time do I spend with my mentor?
- What do I discuss with my mentor? Is it okay to talk to them about nonwork-related things?
- How do I make sure we're making progress toward a goal together?
- My mentor isn't giving me what I need. How do I tell them? Do I even tell them?
- I want to keep working with my mentor after the time commitment is over. Is it acceptable to continue working with them after our originally agreed upon time frame?

In this chapter, I'll guide you on how to develop and maintain a successful mentor-mentee relationship, covering the previous questions.

One of the keys to a successful mentor-mentee relationship is relationship nurturing. We'll discuss what it means to nurture your relationship with your mentor, including setting expectations, regular check-ins, and being open to receiving feedback.

Effective communication is the foundation of any strong relationship, especially in a mentor-mentee one. We'll cover how to communicate effectively with your mentor, including how to ask for feedback and how to communicate your goals and expectations. We'll also discuss the different types of communication necessary to maintain a strong mentor-mentee relationship.

At some point, you may recognize that the relationship has run its course. Knowing when to retire from a relationship is an important skill to learn. We'll provide guidance on how to recognize the signs that it's time to move on and how to do so respectfully.

Whether they are a mentor where you work or a mentor outside of where you work, we will discuss the difference in both dynamics, relationship nurturing, and your responsibilities as a mentee to drive the relationship.

Navigating the mentorship journey as a goal-oriented individual can sometimes blur the lines between the mentor-mentee relationship and the professional objectives you strive to achieve. It's natural to intertwine the two, but always remember that your mentor is not the ultimate goal itself. Instead, your mentor serves as a guide on the path to achieving milestones and growth. This perspective shift can help you approach your interactions in a more balanced and fruitful manner, focusing on the insights and guidance your mentor provides.

> *Remember that your mentor is not the ultimate goal itself. Instead, your mentor serves as a guide on the path to achieving milestones and growth.*

Many of my mentors were introduced to me at a time where I needed their exact skill set. A colleague introduced to me a woman named Kimberly. Kimberly was an executive for some of the largest companies with global recognition and had a passion for mentoring women. Her expertise in relationship building, human resources, and DEI (diversity, equity, and inclusion) departments inside large companies was essential to helping me develop the next prototype of The Mentor Method platform in its infancy.

Kimberly and I originally were focusing on improving my product functionality but expanded the relationship to understanding the broader sales landscape for the business I was in. This introduction took place in 2018, and now we're still in touch frequently. I've had personal conversations with her about life as a leader, a woman executive, how she balances work and family, how she enjoys her consulting business, and more. She has been a guiding light in tough times, but had I treated my early interactions with Kimberly as transactional and only focused on the immediate goal, this multiyear relationship wouldn't exist today.

Staying open to the natural evolution of the relationship with your mentor will allow you to grow together. Which means as their career evolves, there may be more opportunities to help you expand yours as well. And as you grow, they're able to reflect and learn from your journey as well.

My best mentor relationships have been the ones that grow over time. They become more in depth, the conversations become more tailored as we get to know each other, and the degree of explanation required to make a point reduces, which allows more time for a fruitful conversation. These relationships have evolved from strictly professional to being true friends. That wouldn't have happened if I hadn't stayed open to the journey.

There is an old saying a few mentors told me when I was starting my company and was unsure of how to build my team: "If you want to go fast, go alone. If you want to go far, go together." You can find quick answers to your questions through Google and a business coach. But if you want real advice from a real expert who's invested in your well-being and not a transactional check, build your network of mentors and prioritize those relationships.

Ten Behavioral Indicators of a Successful Mentee

The definition of success varies for each person, shaped by their unique perspective. There are distinct behaviors and qualities shared by accomplished CEOs and thriving mentees. Integrating these attributes in a manner that aligns with your authentic self can foster stronger mentor relationships and enhance your leadership abilities. The insights gained throughout this journey contribute to your skill set, leaving a lasting mark on your career trajectory.

Growth-oriented mindset: A successful mentee approaches challenges as opportunities for growth and development. They view setbacks as valuable learning experiences and are not discouraged by initial failures. This mindset fosters resilience, adaptability, and a continuous desire to improve. Let's say a mentee is working on a complex project that hits a roadblock. They analyze the situation, seek advice from their mentor, and explore alternative solutions. They are open to constructive feedback and use it to refine their approach, ultimately turning the setback into a chance to enhance their problem-solving skills.

Proactive communication in between meetings and follow-up: A successful mentee maintains open communication with their mentor between meetings. They initiate conversations to share updates on their progress, schedule conversations, seek advice on challenges, share articles related to their conversations or topics mentioned, and set the pace of communications. After a meeting, they follow up with a summary email within 24 hours of the meeting, outlining action items discussed and the steps they plan to take.

Resilience and adaptability: Imagine a mentee working on a complex project that hits unexpected roadblocks. A successful mentee reaches out to their mentor for advice on overcoming obstacles. They might adapt their approach based on the mentor's insights and continue to drive the project forward.

Continuous learning mindset: A successful mentee eager to enhance their industry knowledge might share an industry-specific article with their mentor. They could ask their mentor for insights on the article's implications and discuss how the new information might influence their approach to a current project. They actively seek recommendations for books, articles, or courses related to their field and share insights gained from their self-directed learning with their mentor. This behavior shows their commitment to continuous improvement.

Effective communication skills: A successful mentee communicates authentically with an open mind and willingness to connect. During a mentorship meeting, a successful mentee could provide a concise update on their recent accomplishments, any challenges faced, and the steps taken to address those challenges. This focused communication ensures that the mentor is well informed and can provide relevant guidance.

Active listening and receptiveness: A successful mentee actively engages in conversations with their mentor, demonstrating that they value the mentor's insights. During a meeting, they ask clarifying questions, paraphrase the mentor's advice to ensure understanding, and later follow up with a summary email, highlighting key takeaways.

Accountability and goal setting: A successful mentee takes ownership of their professional development by setting specific goals with their mentor. They provide regular updates on their progress and setbacks, seeking guidance on overcoming obstacles. For example, they might discuss their goal of enhancing presentation skills and share their efforts to join a public speaking club.

- **Adopting constructive feedback:** When receiving constructive feedback from their mentor, a successful mentee responds with a growth mindset. They take the feedback as an opportunity for improvement rather than becoming defensive. For example, if their mentor suggests refining time management, the mentee actively seeks strategies to implement and demonstrates progress in subsequent interactions.

- **Resourcefulness and problem solving:** Faced with a challenging work situation, a successful mentee showcases resourcefulness. They consult with their mentor, outlining the issue and their initial attempts to address it. Seeking guidance, they collaboratively brainstorm potential solutions with their mentor and later implement the recommended approach, demonstrating effective problem-solving skills.

- **Respect for boundaries and time management:** A successful mentee values their mentor's time and maintains a respectful approach. They always arrive on time for meetings, stick to the allocated time frame, and avoid extending conversations beyond what was agreed upon. This approach ensures that both the mentor's and mentee's time is used efficiently.

Incorporating these attributes can significantly enhance your experience as a mentee and the overall success of your mentorship relationship. By actively engaging, setting clear goals, showing appreciation, and staying receptive to feedback, you contribute to a thriving mentorship partnership that propels your professional growth forward. Mentorship is a collaborative journey, and your commitment plays a pivotal role in achieving meaningful results.

> *By actively engaging, setting clear goals, showing appreciation, and staying receptive to feedback, you contribute to a thriving mentorship partnership that propels your professional growth forward.*

Questions to Ask Yourself When Meeting with Your Mentor

Effective mentorship thrives on a two-way exchange of knowledge, experiences, and insights. As a mentee, your role goes beyond passively receiving advice; it involves active engagement, reflection, and preparation. Before each meeting with your mentor, taking the time to ask yourself meaningful questions can significantly enhance the value you and your mentor derive from the interaction.

Reflecting on Progress and Growth

As you prepare for a mentorship meeting, carve out time to review your personal and professional updates that took place since your last interaction. Acknowledging your growth and identifying areas where you've applied mentorship insights will help you gain a clearer perspective on your development.

- What achievements or milestones have I reached since our last meeting?
- How have I applied the advice and insights from my mentor in my personal and professional life?
- What challenges did I face, and how did I navigate them based on my mentor's guidance?
- In what ways have I grown or developed since our last interaction?
- Can I provide examples of how my mentor's advice directly influenced my decision-making and actions?

Measuring Impact and Learning

Consider the impact of your mentor's guidance on your development. This self-assessment enables you to gauge the tangible benefits of your mentorship and identify areas where further improvement is needed.

- What specific lessons have I learned as a result of my mentor's guidance?

- How have I improved or developed my skills based on the recommendations from my mentor?
- Can I share examples where I applied my mentor's advice and observed positive outcomes?
- What new insights or perspectives have I gained from my mentor's guidance?
- How have I adapted my approach to challenges based on the insights provided by my mentor?

Identifying Knowledge Gaps

Consider areas where you require additional guidance, clarity, or skill development. Pinpointing your knowledge gaps and curating targeted questions will help steer the conversation in a direction that aligns with your current needs and aspirations.

- Are there any specific areas or topics where I don't feel confident in my knowledge base or experience level?
- Do I need guidance on immediate decisions I'm currently facing?
- Are there aspects of my career or personal development that I feel uncertain about?
- What skills or competencies do I believe would benefit from my mentor's expertise?
- Can I identify any hurdles or obstacles that could benefit from my mentor's insights?

Setting Intention and Direction

Craft a clear agenda for the upcoming mentorship meeting. Determine the specific topics you'd like to address during your conversation. Having a well-defined intention for the meeting not only keeps you focused but also enables your mentor to provide targeted guidance faster.

- What are the key topics or goals I want to discuss with my mentor during our upcoming meeting?
- Are there specific projects or initiatives I'd like to seek advice on?
- What recent experiences or challenges are relevant to my mentor's expertise?

- How can I align the mentorship meeting with my current career aspirations?
- Are there any areas where I'm seeking a different perspective or fresh insights from my mentor?

How Are You Using Their Advice?

Evaluate your execution of the advice and recommendations provided by your mentor. Sharing these experiences with your mentor proactively demonstrates your commitment to maximizing the value of their mentorship. While your progress is not a reflection on the mentor, as someone who mentors professionals and entrepreneurs, it feels good to know that you're leaving a positive impact on your mentee and enabling them to achieve their goals. Keeping track of how you're using their advice may motivate your mentor to come up with more suggestions, now that they've seen you'll apply what they share with you during your meetings.

- How have I integrated the advice provided by my mentor into my professional practices?
- Can I share examples where I encountered obstacles and used my mentor's insights to overcome them?
- Have I achieved any wins or milestones as a result of applying my mentor's guidance?
- What challenges or setbacks did I face while implementing my mentor's recommendations?
- In what ways has my mentor's advice led to positive changes or improvements in my approach?

Approaching mentorship meetings with a self-assessment mindset enhances the overall effectiveness of the partnership. By reflecting on your progress, measuring the impact of guidance, identifying knowledge gaps, setting clear

Mentorship is a collaborative relationship that thrives on your active participation and proactive engagement.

intentions, and evaluating advice implementation, you establish a solid foundation for meaningful interactions with your mentor. Mentorship is a collaborative relationship that thrives on your active participation and proactive engagement. By asking yourself thoughtful questions, you unlock the full potential of mentorship and pave the way for continuous growth and development.

Preparing for Your Mentor Meetings: What to Bring and How to Prepare

Approaching mentor meetings with a well-structured plan and thoughtful preparation is essential for ensuring productive and meaningful interactions. Effective preparation goes beyond simply showing up for your meetings—it involves active participation, staying organized, and engaging in discussions that contribute to your personal and professional growth. By proactively defining the purpose of the meeting and arranging your thoughts, you can fully leverage your mentor's expertise and guidance. Again, your goal is to make the interactions as simple as possible. Preparing ahead of time ensures you're able to accomplish that.

Embrace authenticity and genuine conversations. Not every minute of your meeting needs to be centered on work-related matters. Some of my most powerful mentor relationships have stemmed from discussions about the broader world, their families, my family, and life in general—all of which tie into our work. Building a meaningful connection becomes challenging if the conversation revolves solely around work topics.

To ensure your mentor meetings generate positive results, bear in mind the following guidelines and considerations: define the meeting's purpose, research and gather insights, prepare relevant materials, craft an agenda, prepare for potential questions and challenges, be open to feedback, set clear objectives, and create a comfortable environment.

Define the Meeting's Purpose

Meeting without a clear purpose benefits neither you nor your mentor. Before your meeting, clearly outline your objectives. What do you hope to discuss or achieve? Perhaps you need guidance on a challenge, want to chat about career aspirations, or share project updates. Establishing a purpose not only sets expectations but ensures both parties know what to expect. If there's no clear objective, it's better to reschedule the meeting to respect your mentor's time. Remember, each meeting should lean on your mentor's expertise to aid your growth.

Here are some possible focuses for your meetings:

- Leadership development: Are you looking to refine specific leadership skills? Your mentor can advise on strategies, communication methods, and decision-making.
- Industry insight: Discuss emerging trends and new technologies with your mentor to keep current on the latest in your field.
- Networking: If you aim to broaden your network, your mentor can offer tips on effective networking, making connections, and sustaining those relationships.
- Workplace dynamics: This is a good starting point if you want to build strategies for a better work environment, managing conflicts, or collaborating effectively.
- Spotting opportunities: Your mentor can advise on recognizing and seizing opportunities in your industry, from networking to skill development.
- Career transitions: Considering a career shift? Get insights into the process, challenges, and potential routes from your mentor.
- Growth planning: A conversation could revolve around crafting a development plan, detailing your aspirations, steps, and growth timeline, with your mentor guiding the way.

Research and Gather Insights

Research the topics you plan to discuss during the meeting. Familiarize yourself with relevant industry trends, best practices, or any recent developments that pertain to your discussion points. This knowledge not only demonstrates your commitment but also allows for more informed conversations, where you feel confident and equipped to engage in the conversation as an active participant. Your mentor will appreciate your effort to come prepared with insightful questions and context.

Prepare Relevant Materials

Consider whether there are any materials or documents that can enhance the discussion. If you're working on a project, bring along project updates, reports, or presentations that provide an overview of your progress and challenges. Sharing relevant materials allows your mentor to better understand the context and offer tailored advice that aligns with your goals.

Materials to prepare include:

- Work samples or portfolios;
- Action plans or proposals;
- Research findings;
- Goals and objectives list;
- Questions and discussion points; and
- Timeline and progress tracker.

Craft an Agenda

Craft a meeting agenda to highlight the primary topics you'd like to address and share it with your mentor beforehand. Be sure to incorporate the questions you intend to ask, any challenges you're facing, and the type of guidance you're seeking. This preplanned structure guarantees you touch on all important aspects, maximizing the time with your mentor. A well-thought-out agenda demonstrates your appreciation for their time and your dedication to a fruitful dialogue.

Here is a sample agenda, tailored for a mentee who is a magazine writer.

Email subject: Meeting agenda for our upcoming meeting

Hi [mentor's name],

How was your weekend? I'm looking forward to our meeting on [date and time] and learning more about you. Below is the agenda I've put together for our upcoming discussion:

Agenda:

- Progress update: Briefly share recent achievements and milestones in my writing projects. Recap of the list of potential topics and projects for growth we discussed in our last meeting.

- Article challenges: Discuss specific challenges I'm facing in crafting articles that receive over 1,000 views the first day of publishing. Example is attached for reference.
  o How do I create successful article openings?
  o How do you overcome writer's block?
  o What do you recommend on pitching unique and compelling article concepts?

I'm looking forward to our conversation and greatly appreciate your willingness to share your expertise.
Best,
[Your name]

Prepare for Potential Questions and Challenges

Conversations with your mentor will be interactive, and they may pose questions to better support your development. Think ahead about possible inquiries related to your challenges or decisions you're facing. While they may not ask these exact questions, this preparatory exercise ensures you're well equipped for the conversation. If a question surprises you, responding with, "That's an insightful question. I need to reflect on it further," or, "Interesting question. While I don't have a detailed answer ready, here's my initial thought," is perfectly acceptable.
Potential questions from your mentor include:

- How have you been since our last meeting?
- Could you update me on the progress of the project you were working on?
- What specific challenges or roadblocks have you encountered recently?
- Have you had opportunities to implement the advice we discussed previously?
- How are you balancing your current workload and any personal commitments?
- Have you considered exploring new skills or areas of expertise that align with your career path?
- Could you share an example of a situation where you successfully applied a new strategy or approach?

- How do you envision your career evolving in the next few months or years?

Be Open to Feedback

Approach the meeting with an open mind and a willingness to learn from their insights. Feedback is a valuable tool for growth and development.

Mentors provide guidance based on their experiences, and sometimes this feedback may include areas for improvement. Approach the meeting with an open mind and a willingness to learn from their insights. Feedback is a valuable tool for growth and development.

Set Clear Objectives

Establish clear objectives for the meeting. What do you hope to achieve by the end of the conversation? Whether it's gaining clarity on a career decision, receiving advice on a project, or setting short-term goals, having clear objectives helps guide the conversation and ensures you leave the meeting with actionable takeaways.

Using the example of a magazine writer preparing for a meeting with their mentor, their objectives could be:

- Feedback on an article pitch: Seek guidance and feedback on an article pitch that the writer is developing. Discuss the angle, relevance, and potential sources to ensure the pitch is compelling and aligned with the magazine's target audience.
- Career development strategy: Explore strategies for advancing in the field of magazine writing. Discuss opportunities for building a strong portfolio, expanding writing skills, and identifying potential areas of specialization within the industry.
- Navigating editorial challenges: Share insights about any challenges faced while working on recent articles, such as handling tight deadlines or addressing specific editorial requirements. Seek advice on effectively managing these challenges while maintaining high-quality writing standards.

Create a Comfortable Environment

Whether the meeting is in person or virtually, create a comfortable and conducive environment. Minimize distractions and choose a location where you can focus on the discussion. If meeting virtually, ensure your technology is functioning well and you have a stable Internet connection.

▩   ▩   ▩

Getting ready for meetings with your mentors is just as significant as the meetings themselves. Implementing these strategies primes you for success, eliminates uncertainty in managing the meeting, and creates space for both you and your mentor to engage in enjoyable conversations. Now that you're equipped for your meetings, let's turn our attention to communicating with your mentor. Whether you're wondering about how to forge a closer relationship with your mentor, what boundaries to set, or how to handle the reciprocal nature of mentorship, the next chapter will guide you on how to effectively communicate with your mentor while cultivating a valuable relationship.

9

Fostering a Powerful Connection: The Secrets of Effective Mentor Communication

NAVIGATING THE INTRICATE dance of communication within a mentorship relationship is both an art and a science. It is the cornerstone that supports the weight of this dynamic partnership, transforming simple interactions into a rich tapestry of shared knowledge, wisdom, and mutual respect. Mastering the language of effective communication with your mentor is the key to unlocking the full potential of this powerful alliance.

> *Mastering the language of effective communication with your mentor is the key to unlocking the full potential of this powerful alliance.*

In this chapter, we will explore the principles and best practices that constitute meaningful mentor-mentee dialogue. From understanding the subtleties of non-verbal communication to learning the art of active listening and thoughtful questioning, we will guide you through the essential skills required to foster a strong and enduring connection with your mentor. By the end of this journey, you will be equipped with the tools necessary to cultivate a mentorship that not only facilitates your professional growth but also contributes significantly to your personal development.

Engaging with Your Mentor through Thoughtful Questions

Effective mentor meetings are collaborative, with your questions playing a key role in guiding the conversation. Thoughtful and relevant questions not only showcase your engagement but also open up valuable learning opportunities. Aim to explore your mentor's experiences, challenges, and decision-making processes through your questions. Ask about their career path, defining moments in their journey, and the lessons they took away from those experiences.

Focus on open-ended questions to foster rich, meaningful conversations. Instead of yes-or-no questions, craft your questions to prompt your mentor to share their thoughts and insights extensively.

When creating your list of questions during your meeting with your mentor, consider the following: learn about their journey, industry insights, practical insights, and learning from experience.

Learn about Their Journey

Learning from your mentor's personal experiences is a deeply rewarding aspect of mentorship. To gain insights into their career journey, you should ask questions about key milestones, important decisions they made, and periods of significant growth. Here are some questions that can help steer your conversations with your mentor:

- Could you share a turning point in your career and the lessons you gained from it?
- What were some challenges you faced early in your career, and how did you navigate them?
- How have your experiences shaped your approach to professional development?

Industry Insights

Gain insights from your mentor's understanding of industry dynamics. Ask for their opinions on current trends, recent innovations, and upcoming opportunities in your field. Ask them about the changes they've observed in the industry over the years and where they predict it will go in the future. You might ask:

- What current developments in our industry do you find most intriguing?
- Could you identify any emerging trends or potential opportunities in our field?
- How has the industry shifted since you first started your career?
- Are there specific skills or areas of expertise you think are becoming more valuable?

Practical Insights

Invite your mentor to provide practical insights by asking about their everyday routines and methods for making decisions. This will give you a clearer picture of what your future career might entail. Possible questions include:

- How do you prioritize tasks and ensure your time is used efficiently?
- What factors influence your decision when selecting projects to work on?
- Could you describe what you enjoy least about your job?
- What does a typical day look like for you, both on good and bad days?
- What techniques do you employ to keep yourself organized and manage your time effectively?
- How do you tackle decision-making when faced with multiple projects or opportunities?
- What approaches have you found most useful in balancing your professional and personal life priorities?

Learning from Experience

Ask your mentor about the times they faced setbacks or made mistakes in their career, and how they turned those situations into learning experiences. This will give you a more comprehensive understanding of growth and development. Learning from both successes and failures can provide a well-rounded perspective on growth.

Learning from both successes and failures can provide a well-rounded perspective on growth.

- What advice can you offer on avoiding common pitfalls and maximizing learning opportunities?
- How have you integrated the lessons learned from both successes and failures into your ongoing growth journey?
- What's your approach to maintaining a growth mindset during difficult times?

Give First: Cultivate a Giving Mindset

The foundation of a successful mentor-mentee relationship is reciprocity. Approach the mentorship with a mindset of giving as much as you receive. While mentors offer guidance, mentees can provide fresh perspectives, innovative ideas, and insights into emerging trends.

Share your own experiences and lessons learned. Don't hesitate to offer assistance to your mentor where your skills and knowledge align. Be willing to provide feedback, share relevant articles, or introduce them to connections in your network. This giving mindset contributes to a collaborative partnership where both parties learn and grow from each other's contributions.

An Example of Giving First

Kyle is an aspiring sales professional with a passion for establishing multiyear brand partnerships, who sought mentorship to elevate his expertise and expand his horizons. From the beginning, Kyle embraced the "give first" philosophy, setting a strong foundation for his connection with his mentor.

In one of their monthly sessions, Kyle discovered that his mentor, Nadia, was keen on devising new strategies to boost brand collaborations within her athletic leisure clothing company. Tapping into his expertise, Kyle suggested an analysis of recent successful brand collaborations he'd observed in his sector. He drafted an initial report outlining current trends, emerging opportunities, and growth areas that aligned with Nadia's aspirations. Whenever he found articles or case studies pertinent to their discussions, he shared them with Nadia. This proactive sharing enhanced their discussions with fresh perspectives.

Aware that his network included professionals with expertise in the problem Nadia was seeking to solve, Kyle connected Nadia with a social media collaboration expert, perfectly aligning with her goals.

Kyle's consistent spirit of giving and sharing set a tone of mutual respect and reciprocity in his interactions with Nadia. As their mentorship journey advanced, Nadia grew to value Kyle's proactive stance and his readiness to share valuable insights. This not only solidified their bond but also highlighted Kyle's dedication to a mutually enriching partnership.

Kyle's story highlights the importance of contributing positively to the mentor-mentee relationship. He leveraged his know-how, experiences, and contacts, reinforcing his investment in Nadia's success as her mentee and crafting a rewarding mentorship ambiance.

Lessons Learned

Below is what Kyle, the mentee, did right in the story:

- Embraced the giving mindset: Kyle understood the importance of giving as much as receiving in a mentorship relationship.
- Proactive contribution: He proposed a detailed analysis of recent successful brand partnerships, showcasing his initiative to actively contribute insights to their discussions.
- Shared relevant resources: Kyle proactively shared articles and case studies that enriched their discussions and provided fresh perspectives.
- Strategic networking: Recognizing Nadia's interest, Kyle introduced her to a contact specializing in influencer collaborations, demonstrating his willingness to leverage his network for mutual benefit.
- Demonstrated commitment: Kyle consistently contributed insights, resources, and connections, showcasing his dedication to a meaningful partnership. His consistent giving mindset fostered a sense of reciprocity, strengthening the collaborative nature of their mentorship.

- Strengthened the relationship: His proactive and collaborative approach deepened their mentorship dynamic over time.
- Value-added contributions: By offering analysis and relevant resources, Kyle showcased his ability to provide valuable insights.
- Aligned with mentor's goals: His actions aligned with Nadia's interests and goals, making his contributions meaningful and relevant.

These actions collectively showcased Kyle's commitment to actively engaging in the mentorship and contributing to a mutually beneficial relationship with his mentor, Nadia.

Boundaries with Your Mentor: Navigating Openness and Closeness

Establishing and maintaining appropriate boundaries promotes a healthy and productive mentorship. Mentorship thrives on open communication and sharing, but there are certain topics and levels of closeness that should be approached with caution. In this section, we will explore the nuances of setting boundaries with your mentor, including what subjects to discuss and the depth of your connection.

What to Talk about and Not Talk About

Open and honest communication is vital in mentorship. Yet, it's important to be mindful of the topics you discuss. Some areas are best for professional development discussions, while others may infringe upon personal boundaries. Here's what you should and shouldn't talk about:

What to Share

- Career goals and progress: Discussing professional aspirations and progress is fundamental to the mentorship journey.
- Challenges and roadblocks: Address obstacles and seek advice on potential solutions.
- Skill development: Discuss improving or acquiring skills.
- Industry trends: Talk about current industry trends and shifts in your field.

- Networking and opportunities: Inquire about networking events and potential professional connections.

What to Avoid

- Personal life: Avoid sharing intimate details of your personal life unless it's relevant to your professional growth.
- Sensitive topics: Steer clear of discussions that involve political, religious, or controversial matters.
- Negative remarks: Focus on constructive conversations rather than negative remarks about colleagues, company leadership, or competitors.

Assessing the Depth of Your Mentorship Connection: Finding the Right Balance

The depth of your connection may evolve over time. It's important to assess the level of rapport to ensure conversations are enriching without crossing boundaries. Consider the following to gauge your closeness:

- Frequency of interaction: Frequent interactions can foster a closer bond.
- Shared experiences: Engaging in discussions beyond professional topics can signify a deeper connection.
- Level of comfort: A growing comfort level may indicate a stronger connection.
- Mutual interest: A mentor's genuine interest in your well-being can be a sign of a supportive relationship.

Finding a balance between professionalism and authenticity is key to effective boundary setting. Although openness is encouraged, the focus should be on your professional development. Both you and your mentor can navigate the boundaries together to create a growth-oriented environment.

Finding a balance between professionalism and authenticity is key to effective boundary setting. Although openness is encouraged, the focus should be on your professional development.

When uncertain, follow your mentor's lead on closeness and confirm it aligns with your internal boundaries. I've had mentors who preferred strictly professional conversations and others who were more open, sharing personal details over a longer time frame. In both cases, the relationships were maintained and valued. Understanding and managing boundaries in your mentorship is integral to enhancing your interactions and fostering a respectful and enriching relationship.

The Five Stages of a Mentor Relationship

Cultivating a solid and powerful mentor-mentee bond is a process that can develop gradually. Venturing through this process can occasionally feel somewhat unclear, particularly in gauging the degree of rapport or familiarity with your mentor. This is where the notion of the five stages of growing closer to a mentor becomes relevant. Identifying your current position in this progression can lessen apprehension and foster a more relaxed environment for your dialogues, enabling you to concentrate on the priceless wisdom and direction provided by your mentor.

Stage 1: Initial Connection

In the early stages of mentorship, you find yourself forming an initial connection. Here, you're beginning to know each other, with discussions often centered on your professional history, aspirations, and interests. This is the foundational period where the dynamics of the mentor-mentee relationship are shaped, similar to the opening chapter of a book that introduces the main characters and sets the stage for the unfolding story.

Stage 2: Sharing Experiences

Following this, you move into the stage of sharing experiences. This is the time when you start to open up about your triumphs and difficulties, and your mentor shares relevant anecdotes from their own journey. This sharing brings a human touch to the relationship and creates a bond rooted in empathy and mutual understanding.

Stage 3: Seeking Guidance

Next, you enter the stage of seeking guidance, where your conversations are more focused on soliciting advice and solutions for your professional challenges. Drawing from their wealth of experience, your mentor provides valuable insights and encourages you to consider your options carefully. It's beneficial to come prepared with specific questions and situations to fully leverage the wisdom your mentor offers.

Stage 4: Personal Insights

The fourth stage is about exchanging personal insights. This is a deeper, more intimate phase where discussions go beyond your professional journey and touch on your values, motivations, and long-term objectives. Conversations may extend to how your career intersects with your personal life and overarching goals, thereby facilitating a comprehensive understanding of each other.

Stage 5: Long-Term Relationship

Here, you've built a solid bond characterized by mutual trust and shared experiences. Conversations are multifaceted, covering both professional and personal areas, and your mentor has become a trusted advisor and potentially a lifelong professional confidant.

Understanding the five stages of mentor-mentee relationships can guide you in tailoring your communication style and setting the right expectations. While the pace of progression through these stages varies, with some relationships deepening over time and others remaining more surface level, recognizing your current stage helps you focus on what's most beneficial at that point, whether it's seeking advice or sharing personal insights. This awareness can enhance the ease and value of your interactions, contributing significantly to your personal and professional development. Embrace the unique journey and bond that you are forming with your mentor as your relationship evolves.

Recognizing When It's Time to Retire a Mentorship Relationship

The dynamic between a mentor and mentee is a valuable one, providing guidance, insights, and a platform for learning. However, just as mentorships have the potential to blossom and flourish, there may come a point where the relationship has run its course. The top CEOs all understand needing to make the best decisions for their company. This can include deciding when it's time to change direction, restructure the team, and evaluate what's helping them be successful without looking back or having regrets. Recognizing when it's time to retire a mentorship relationship is an essential skill that allows both parties to move forward in their respective paths with clarity and respect.

Signs That It's Time to Move On

- Lack of alignment: A shift in goals or professional direction that no longer match your mentor's expertise is a sign that the relationship may have reached its natural conclusion.
- Diminishing impact: If the mentor's advice is becoming repetitive or isn't contributing to your growth, it might be time to part ways.
- Limited availability: A successful mentorship requires consistent communication. A significant decrease in your mentor's availability may reduce the effectiveness of the relationship.
- Different perspectives: Continuous divergent viewpoints or approaches can hinder growth, as a mentorship should foster constructive discussions, not conflicts.
- Achievement of goals: Reaching the goals set with your mentor's help may mean the relationship has served its purpose, and continuing it might lead to complacency.

Retiring the Relationship Respectfully

Initiate a conversation: When you decide it's time to end the mentorship, have an open and honest discussion with your mentor. Thank them for their guidance, and explain why you've made this decision.

Show respect and recognize the positive impact the relationship has had on your development. If the relationship has reached its natural end given an agreed-upon time frame, thank them and do not continue with further explanation. Make sure you connect with them on LinkedIn, and if you have a routine updates newsletter you share, add them to the list to receive that as well.

Focus on growth: Highlight that your decision is based on your evolving objectives and aspirations. Explain that you're seeking new experiences and different viewpoints to further your professional path.

Offer appreciation: Show gratitude for the time and effort your mentor has invested in your development. Thank them for the support and insights provided throughout the mentorship.

Stay connected: The end of a formal mentorship doesn't mean losing contact. Express your desire to maintain an informal relationship, including occasional catch-ups or sharing updates.

Maintain professionalism: Focus the conversation on your decision and reasons, avoiding any blame or negative sentiments that could tarnish the positive aspects of the relationship.

When you identify that it's time to conclude a mentorship, it demonstrates your growth and self-awareness, highlighting your ability to assess your needs, objectives, and evolving career path with maturity. Handling this transition with respect and professionalism not only preserves the positive aspects of the mentorship for your professional journey but also keeps the door open for future collaborations. Remember, concluding a mentorship that has fulfilled its purpose is a progressive step that opens up new possibilities, introduces fresh perspectives, and brings in new mentors, all of which can significantly contribute to your pursuit of success.

▩ ▩ ▩

Engaging your mentor through thoughtful conversations allows for a deeper understanding, ultimately fostering growth. A giving mindset contributes to a balanced and fruitful relationship, benefiting both parties involved. Establishing and respecting boundaries is important to maintain a healthy balance between openness and closeness, ensuring the mentorship remains respectful and productive. Understanding the five stages of a mentor relationship helps you navigate each phase effectively, learning and adapting as the relationship evolves. Implementing these key principles will enhance your mentorship experience, leading to a rewarding journey of shared insights, mutual growth, and positive impact.

In the following chapter, we'll examine how mentorship needs shift throughout your career progression and the ways you can engage your board of mentors during various phases such as the early stages, mid-level, industry transitions, and as an experienced professional to enhance your mentor relationships.

10

Navigating Mentor Relationships throughout Your Career

WHEN YOU'RE BUILDING your network of mentors, the stage of life you're in can influence the type of mentors you need and how you interact with them. This chapter will outline how to collaborate with different types of mentors, the roles they may occupy, and how your questions may change based on your career level and life stage. This information is particularly relevant for professionals who have faced obstacles or haven't yet realized the transformative power of mentorship.

While it might seem beneficial to gather a diverse range of mentors all at once, this approach can be counterproductive in the long term, as covered in Chapter 3. It's important to remain focused and seek mentors only when you have the capacity to engage with them. Managing more than three mentor relationships at once can be overwhelming and may prevent you from fully benefiting from each relationship. It's often more effective to deepen your connections with your current mentors.

> *Managing more than three mentor relationships at once can be overwhelming and may prevent you from fully benefiting from each relationship.*

In this chapter, we will explore mentorship at various career stages:

First-time entering the workforce: This applies if you entered the workforce within the last two years or are preparing to do so, or if you have not held a full-time professional job before.

Entering a new industry: Transitioning into a new industry can be more intimidating than being new to the workforce. You may worry about repeating past mistakes, feel uncertain about what to expect, and question your career decision, or you may feel excited about what your next chapter will entail. Regardless of the outcome, embrace the courage it took to switch industries, and seek mentors who will clarify your new environment and guide you in making informed decisions.

Mid-level: With six to ten years of professional experience, you have a stronger understanding of your strengths and may feel that you've outgrown your previous roles. As you take on more leadership responsibilities and plan for the next decade, mentors can help you identify your next steps, consider potential career shifts, and expand your network.

Experienced in your career but new to mentorship: Even seasoned professionals who might feel they've overlooked mentorship opportunities can still reap immense benefits from such relationships. Whether confronting new challenges, reinforcing your position, or advancing within your established role, the advantages of mentorship are consistently substantial at any stage in your career.

Regardless of your career stage, mentorship is accessible to you, offering valuable support and opportunities for growth. Remember, it's never too late to seek mentorship. In this chapter, we'll guide you on how to find mentors that align with your career path. Cultivating a network of mentors requires patience, but the rewards are significant. By the close of this chapter, you will know how to maximize your mentor relationships based on your career phase.

Navigating Mentorship for Early Career Professionals

Stepping into your professional journey can be an exhilarating yet sometimes unclear venture, especially within your first one to two years after entering the workforce. The support and wisdom of mentors can significantly ease this transition, supporting you in tackling challenges, making well-informed choices, and propelling your career forward. This section is dedicated to helping those new to the workforce understand how to effectively engage with various mentor types to sculpt their career trajectory.

Company Insider Mentor

Ideal mentor roles: Mid-level colleagues in your department or individuals who have been with the company for a minimum of five years.
   Questions to Ask

- How can I gain a strong understanding of the company culture and integrate into the team effectively?
- What are some unwritten rules or nuances that could help me succeed in this organization?
- Could you share your experiences transitioning from a newcomer to a tenured team member within the company?

Skill Master Mentor

Ideal mentor roles: Colleagues distinguished in skills pertinent to your role, such as an adept presenter or a skilled project manager.
   Questions to Ask

- How did you develop your expertise in [specific skill]? Any tips for someone starting out?
- Could you recommend resources or training programs to help me enhance my [specific skill] proficiency?
- How can I balance developing this skill with other areas of professional growth?

The Money-minded Mentor

Ideal mentor roles: Professionals who are skilled in financial management and have successfully navigated the financial aspects of their career.

Questions to Ask

- What strategies do you suggest for managing personal finances and making sound financial decisions early in my career?
- How can I negotiate my compensation effectively while maintaining a positive relationship with my employer?
- What are some key financial milestones I should be aiming for in my first few years of work?

The Industry Mentor

Ideal mentor roles: Professionals with significant experience in your industry, preferably in roles more advanced than your current position.

Questions to Ask

- What are the current trends and developments in our industry that I should be aware of?
- How can I leverage my current role to position myself for future growth within the industry?
- Could you share any experiences or challenges you faced early in your career and how you overcame them?

The Network Mentor

Ideal mentor roles: Well-connected professionals who can introduce you to industry peers and facilitate networking opportunities.

Questions to Ask

- How can I effectively build and maintain a professional network that aligns with my career goals?
- Could you provide tips for attending networking events and making meaningful connections?
- How did your networking efforts contribute to your career progression?

The Influential Ally Mentor

Ideal mentor roles: Professionals who advocate for cultures of development and are committed to helping newcomers succeed.

Questions to Ask

- What strategies can I use to build a strong support system within the organization?
- Could you share instances where advocating for yourself or others made a positive impact on your career?
- Does the company have employee resource or affinity groups that you recommend joining?

Peer Mentor

Ideal mentor roles: Colleagues who are one to two years ahead of you in their career journey and can offer relatable insights.

Questions to Ask

- How did you successfully transition from a new hire to becoming more comfortable in your role?
- What challenges did you face in your first years of work, and how did you overcome them?
- How do you balance skill development, networking, and career advancement in these early stages?

In your early career years, the advice and insights from mentors in different areas can play a significant role in shaping your professional path. Don't hesitate to ask for guidance, pose questions, and engage actively with your mentors to maximize these valuable relationships. As you start this journey, mentorship will serve as a reliable guide to help you navigate the complexities of the professional world.

Navigating Mentorship When Entering a New Industry

Stepping into a new industry brings a mix of excitement and challenges as you determine which skills, strengths, and attributes from your current and past experiences will support a successful future in your chosen field.

Mentor guidance can act as your guide, assisting you in unfamiliar territory, helping you make informed decisions, and accelerating your growth.

Mentor guidance can act as your guide, assisting you in unfamiliar territory, helping you make informed decisions, and accelerating your growth.

In this section, we'll look at how you can effectively connect with various mentors to approach the new with less anxiety and more confidence.

Company Insider Mentor

Ideal mentor roles: Seasoned professionals who have an extensive understanding of the industry's inner workings and dynamics.

Questions to Ask

- How can I quickly immerse myself in the industry's culture and become a valued contributor?
- What are some key strategies to network within the industry and establish meaningful connections?
- Could you share insights on successfully transitioning from an outsider to an industry insider?

Skill Master Mentor

Ideal mentor roles: Experts within the industry who have mastered a specific skill relevant to your current or desired role.

Questions to Ask

- How did you become proficient in [specific skill] within this industry, and what steps can I take to follow a similar path?
- Are there any industry-specific training programs or resources you recommend to enhance my skill set?
- How can I leverage my acquired skills to stand out in a competitive industry landscape?

The Money-minded Mentor

Seek out professionals with financial expertise who can assist you in navigating career-related finances within your new industry or provide guidance on developing financial strategies outside of your workplace or industry to help you craft your desired lifestyle.

Questions to Ask

- How can I effectively manage my finances and make informed financial decisions as I navigate this new industry?
- What strategies should I consider for negotiating my compensation package within this specific field?
- Could you provide insights into financial milestones I should aim for as a newcomer to this industry?
- What are a few wise financial investments to make in my future based on what is needed to succeed in this industry?

The Industry Mentor

Ideal mentor roles: Experienced industry veterans who can provide valuable insights into the trends, challenges, and opportunities within the new industry.

Questions to Ask

- What are the current trends and shifts shaping the future of this industry, and how can I position myself to capitalize on them?
- Could you share your experiences overcoming challenges in this industry during your early career stages?
- How do you recommend I align my skill development with the demands and opportunities of this specific industry?

The Network Mentor

Ideal mentor roles: Well-connected professionals who can introduce you to key players, decision-makers, and potential collaborators within the new industry.

Questions to Ask

- How can I build a robust professional network within this industry to foster collaboration and growth?
- Are there specific industry events or associations I should consider engaging with to expand my network?
- Could you share your experiences using networking to your advantage when transitioning to a new industry?

The Influential Ally Mentor

Ideal mentor roles: Professionals who are known advocates for inclusivity within the industry and can guide you in navigating your new environment.

Questions to Ask

- Are there teams, companies, or organizations known for their diverse and inclusive talent management practices?
- What strategies have you employed to build a supportive community and network as a newcomer?
- Could you share instances where your advocacy efforts contributed to positive outcomes within this industry?

Peer Mentor

Ideal mentor roles: Colleagues who have entered the industry recently and have successfully acclimated to the new environment.

Questions to Ask

- How did you manage the transition into this industry, and what tips can you offer for a smooth integration?
- Are there any challenges specific to newcomers in this industry that you've experienced and overcome?
- How do you balance skill development, networking, and rapid industry acclimatization within your first years?

As you begin this new chapter, mentorship from various sectors can play a key role in assisting you through the unknown landscape of a new industry. Take initiative in seeking advice, posing relevant questions, and actively engaging with your mentors. Their wisdom will prove essential as you traverse the unfamiliar territory of your new professional venture, setting the stage for a successful transition and a rewarding career ahead.

Navigating Mentorship for Mid-Level Management Professionals: Charting Your Course

The middle management phase in your career introduces distinct opportunities and is a key time for making strategic career decisions to chart your path forward. As a seasoned professional aiming to elevate your leadership skills and make strategic choices, you're at a pivotal point. This section of the book is designed to help mid-level managers utilize mentorship from various categories to enhance their roles and achieve greater success.

Company Insider Mentor

Ideal mentor roles: Senior leaders well versed in the culture, structure, and dynamics of your organization.

Questions to Ask

- What strategies are effective for building relationships with key stakeholders and decision-makers?
- Could you provide insights on aligning my team's objectives with the company's broader goals?
- How often does the organization promote internally? Are promotions based on skills, tenure, or availability?
- What's the best way to navigate and influence the company's political landscape to foster positive change and progress in my career?

Skill Master Mentor

Ideal mentor roles: Experts proficient in leadership skills, ready to guide you in refining the specific competencies required at this career stage.

Questions to Ask

- How did you develop your leadership style, and what recommendations do you have for refining mine?
- Are there specialized skills, such as negotiation or conflict resolution, I should focus on for success in mid-level management?
- What are your experiences with effective delegation while maintaining an active leadership role?

The Money-Minded Mentor

Ideal mentor roles: Financial experts to assist you in making sound decisions to improve your financial well-being as you progress.

Questions to Ask

- What strategies can I employ to negotiate compensation and benefits that reflect my contributions?
- Are there any financial planning or investment strategies particularly suitable for mid-level managers you would recommend?
- What financial milestones and decisions should I consider at this career stage?

The Industry Mentor

Ideal mentor roles: Seasoned professionals with extensive industry experience who can provide insights into industry trends, challenges, and strategic opportunities.

Questions to Ask

- How can I keep up with industry changes and anticipate shifts that could affect our company's strategies?
- Could you share your experiences in overcoming industry-related challenges at the mid-management level, and the lessons you learned?
- What advice can you offer for aligning my leadership skills with our industry's demands and expectations?
- What senior roles make the best targets given this stage of my career?

The Network Mentor

Ideal mentor roles: Well-connected leaders who can guide you in expanding your professional network and leveraging it to drive business growth.

Questions to Ask

- Are there specific industry events or platforms where mid-level managers can make valuable connections?
- Could you share your experiences in using your network to achieve specific business goals and foster collaboration?

The Influential Ally Mentor

Ideal mentor roles: Advocates for company cultures built on nurturing talent and rising leaders who can guide you in creating a positive and inclusive work environment within your team and organization.
Questions to Ask

- How can I strategically expand my network to include influential peers, mentors, and industry figures at this career stage?
- What strategies have you employed to address inclusivity challenges and advocate for positive change?
- Could you share insights into how diversity affects team performance and overall organizational success?
- Who are the key individuals that could support my next promotional step, and how can I engage with them authentically, avoiding a transactional dynamic?
- I've noticed your connection with [insert name]. Given my interest in a senior role on their team, could we discuss the possibility of an introduction and what information or interactions would make you comfortable facilitating an introduction?

Peer Mentor

Ideal mentor roles: Experienced peers who have successfully navigated mid-level management and can provide valuable insights based on their journey.
Questions to Ask

- How did you transition into mid-level management, and what strategies can you share for effectively managing teams at this stage?
- Are there common challenges or opportunities specific to mid-level management that you've encountered and learned from?
- How can I ensure a balanced approach to leadership, skill enhancement, and networking while thriving as a mid-level manager?

In the mid-level career phase, mentorship plays a key role in personal and professional development. Connect with mentors from various fields, seeking advice and drawing on their knowledge to enhance your leadership capabilities. Proactively ask pertinent questions and learn from their experiences to ensure your success and to amplify your influence within your organization and industry.

Unlocking Mentorship for Experienced Professionals: Empowering Your Journey

For many seasoned professionals, mentorship has often been an overlooked element in their career development. Many people, perhaps including yourself, have felt sidelined in discussions about mentorship. Astonishingly, 63% of women report never having had a formal mentor. This could be attributed to limited opportunities, reduced visibility, or other systemic hurdles. Regardless, it's a new chapter—one where you actively drive your career advancement by seeking the mentorship opportunities you deserve. Whether you're just starting or furthering your profession, mentorship knows no boundaries.

Company Insider Mentor

Ideal mentor roles: Established leaders in your organization who have a comprehensive understanding of the company's culture, structure, and inner workings.

Questions to Ask

- How can I better understand and navigate our organization's culture to further my career and create a meaningful impact?
- What strategies do you recommend for forming valuable relationships and connections within our organization?
- Could you share your experiences in adapting to the evolving dynamics of our workplace while maintaining effectiveness in your leadership?

Skill Master Mentor

Ideal mentor roles: Professionals who have mastered skills integral to your career and can provide guidance on perfecting them.

Questions to Ask

- What methods have you employed to continuously improve and hone your skills as a seasoned professional?
- Could you offer insights on effectively integrating new skills into your existing set of expertise to stay relevant and versatile?
- How can I utilize my existing experience while adopting new skills to thrive in my current role and future endeavors?

The Money-Minded Mentor

Ideal mentor roles: Financially astute professionals who can help you make strategic decisions to secure your financial future.

Questions to Ask

- How can I fine-tune my financial decisions to align with my long-term objectives?
- Are there specific investment strategies that I should consider as an experienced professional?
- Could you share your journey in securing financial stability while navigating through various career transitions and progressions?

The Industry Mentor

Ideal mentor roles: Seasoned professionals with a wealth of knowledge and insights into industry trends, challenges, and strategic opportunities.

Questions to Ask

- How can I effectively utilize my vast experience to stay ahead of industry trends and contribute significantly to strategic discussions?
- Could you provide examples of how your extensive expertise has shaped the decisions and growth of your organization?
- What advice do you have for establishing myself as a key industry player, drawing from my rich experience and insights?

The Network Mentor

Ideal mentor roles: Well-connected leaders who can guide you in growing your professional network to open new avenues for development.
Questions to Ask

- How can I use my years of experience to foster and maintain a robust professional network?
- Are there specific events or platforms that cater to experienced professionals seeking valuable connections?
- Could you offer insights into leveraging my well-established network to unlock new opportunities and collaborative ventures?

The Influential Ally Mentor

Ideal mentor roles: Advocates for inclusivity who can provide guidance on creating an inclusive work environment within your team and organization.
Questions to Ask

- How can I draw from my experience to advocate for diversity and inclusivity within my team, contributing to a positive workplace?
- What strategies have you implemented to address biases and foster inclusivity in your leadership role?
- Could you share your experiences regarding the positive impacts of diversity on team performance and overall organizational success?

Peer Mentor

Ideal mentor roles: Experienced peers who have navigated similar career paths and can offer valuable insights based on their own journeys.
Questions to Ask

- How have you utilized your experience to seamlessly transition into new roles and continue your professional growth?
- What obstacles or opportunities have you encountered, and how have they influenced your career trajectory?

- How can I balance my extensive experience with continuous learning, effective networking, and innovative leadership strategies?

Your career journey, enriched by your wealth of experience, can be significantly enhanced with mentorship serving as a catalyst for growth. Whether you're entering into a new industry, pursuing advancement in your current field, or striving to lead with greater impact, mentorship is a reliable ally.

11

Establishing Mentor Relationships in the Early Days of Entrepreneurship

THE FIRST FIVE years of your entrepreneurial career present different thrills and challenges compared to a corporate career. This chapter will explore the types of mentors helpful during this time in your career and the pros and cons of each for your business.

> Note: Everything in this book applies to you as an entrepreneur. The process of further knowing yourself in Chapter 2 helps you find the right mentors faster, sift through those who aren't a good fit based on the persona you created in Chapter 4, and get the insights you need to make the best decisions for yourself and your company. Following the process for finding mentors also in Chapter 4 is recommended. You'll use a similar approach of conducting meetings and fostering connections from Chapter 6, asking mentors to join you on your entrepreneurial path from Chapter 7, using the power of preparedness for effective meetings from Chapter 8, and genuinely communicate with your mentor from Chapter 9. However, given the nuanced nature of entrepreneurship, this chapter focuses on the types of mentors, questions, and specific details outside of previous chapters that are applicable to your entrepreneur experience.

The information from previous chapters is applicable to entrepreneurs, but this section is specifically for those with early-stage businesses in the first five years of the business's development. The journey of the first five years of building a business, especially as a solo or underrepresented entrepreneur, is unique. While experiences vary, these fundamentals have helped countless entrepreneurs get the resources they need.

When I founded The Mentor Method, despite my educational background studying entrepreneurship from MIT, my career background was in corporate graphic design, and I lacked an entrepreneurial network. The mentors I connected with in the business world became a lifeline to my growth, offering essential insights. Their guidance, paired with my own trial and error, helped me adapt mentorship to my unique learning preferences and personality, ultimately forming me into a more resilient individual, entrepreneur, and business owner.

Opportunities from my network and skills learned through advice from mentors I trust are things I still remember every day. For example, one of my mentors, Joseph, gave me advice on living a fulfilling life outside of work and sharing my story, which I initially avoided. Chris's mentorship provided direct advice that helped me understand my financial projections, securing additional funding and increasing my confidence in investor meetings. Xina, a woman of color in a high-visibility position, balanced ambition, poise, and strategic focus in our mentor-mentee relationship, changing how I viewed myself as a woman leader through her example. These are just a few ways entrepreneurial mentors can empower the early stages of your business.

> Opportunities from my network and skills learned through advice from mentors I trust are things I still remember every day.

As your business grows and you build your team, these relationships can become personal. If you're the CEO or owner, your business is your brainchild, and your emotions are intertwined with its progress. Every day you spend on your business brings you closer to your company's goals. In the early days, when many businesses are short-staffed, you and your business can seem synonymous. Mentors during this time need to understand this to support you best.

When I was in the corporate world, I thought the same type of career mentors would apply to my entrepreneurial journey, but there are key differences.

Successful Entrepreneurship Mentee: Behavioral Characteristics to Excel

To thrive as an entrepreneurship mentee, adopt a proactive, growth-oriented approach and actively engage in your mentorship journey. Specific behavioral traits, detailed in Chapter 8, can help you maximize mentorship benefits and expedite your business development process. By incorporating these characteristics, you'll not only optimize your mentorship experience but also enrich your entrepreneurial journey. Success in the ever-changing business landscape requires open collaboration, targeted action, and a dedication to ongoing enhancement.

Paid Partnerships with Trusted Mentors: Maximizing Value and Vision

Mentorship is based on mutual respect and a shared desire to foster personal and professional growth, but the question of payment can sometimes arise. For example, I joined a start-up accelerator program at the beginning stages of my company that provided access to potential mentors to assist with refining pitches and scaling businesses. In one of my initial meetings, a potential mentor presented me with a list of paid services she could offer. I did not proceed with the relationship.

Traditional mentor-mentee relationships involve learning and growth without financial transactions, and so *you do not pay for mentorship*. However, there are instances where payment might be appropriate when in an entrepreneurial dynamic. For example, if your mentor plays an advisory or consultancy role within your business, financial compensation could be suitable as it acknowledges their time and expertise, aligning their interests with your company's success.

As a new entrepreneur, you might seek specific services or comprehensive guidance that goes beyond typical mentor-mentee interactions. In such cases, a professional agreement with compensation could be beneficial, ensuring you receive the focused support and tailored insights you need in areas such as business strategy, market analysis, or financial planning.

The Roles of Mentors, Freelancers, Advisors, and Board Members in Your Company

Important roles that can foster the growth of your business include entrepreneurial mentors, freelance experts that serve as team members, advisors, and board members. It's important to understand how each of these roles can contribute to your business's development and success.

Mentors, freelance experts, advisors, and board members each bring valuable skills and knowledge that collectively form a solid foundation for your business's growth. Together, they create a support network that can drive transformative results for your venture.

When navigating the complex landscape of entrepreneurship, consider how these roles can work in concert to propel your business forward. Leveraging their combined expertise will prepare you to tackle challenges and seize opportunities, setting you on the path to success.

Now, let's examine the roles of entrepreneurial mentors, freelance expert team members, advisors, and board members in the context of early-stage businesses, drawing on examples from various industries.

An entrepreneurial mentor is an experienced individual who provides guidance, insights, and support to help early-stage entrepreneurs navigate challenges and make informed decisions.

Entrepreneurial mentor: An entrepreneurial mentor is an experienced individual who provides guidance, insights, and support to help early-stage entrepreneurs navigate challenges and make informed decisions. They draw from their own experiences in entrepreneurship to offer valuable lessons.

Example: Sarah is the founder of a sustainable packaging solutions company with a focus on environmental consciousness. She sought guidance from Alex, a successful entrepreneur who launched a similar environmentally conscious product line. Alex shared insights on sourcing eco-friendly materials, forming partnerships with local suppliers, and overcoming regulatory hurdles. Their mentor-mentee relationship helped Sarah guide her company on the right path and avoid potential pitfalls.

Freelance expert: A freelance expert is a specialized professional hired on a project basis to provide expertise in a specific area, complementing the skills of your core team. They can serve as core team members as you generate enough revenue to compensate new team members or as you build your network to find business partners equally as invested in your vision.

Example: Juan, leader of a fashion e-commerce start-up, enlisted the help of Emily, a freelance digital marketing expert specializing in influencer marketing. Emily crafted precise and results-oriented campaigns that enhanced the company's early online presence, driving sales through strategic collaborations with fashion influencers.

Advisor: An advisor is an experienced professional who offers guidance and expertise based on their specialized knowledge. They share insights, industry best practices, and help the company make informed decisions.

Example: A growing pottery company known for its unique hand-crafted ceramic pieces consulted Maria, a seasoned ceramics artist and business owner. Maria advised on optimizing production processes, refining designs to meet customer preferences, and exploring sustainable sourcing practices. Her contributions significantly improved the company's product quality, customer satisfaction, and overall business strategy, helping it stand out in a competitive market.

Board member: A board member holds a formal position on a company's board of directors, providing oversight, governance, and strategic direction to influence major decisions and contribute to the company's long-term success.

Example: A newly launched catering company specializing in farm-to-table events invited Jessica, a seasoned executive with extensive experience in the food and hospitality industry, to join its board of directors. Jessica's background in event management, culinary trends, and strategic business development proved invaluable. Her guidance in crafting unique dining experiences, along with her industry insights, helped the company navigate the competitive landscape of catering and events. By fostering relationships with local farmers and promoting sustainable practices, Jessica helped position the company as a leader in the field, driving success and recognition for their innovative approach to catering.

Building Your Mentor Network

There are eight different types of mentors an early-stage entrepreneur needs across the life span of their business. You do not need every mentor at once. The focus is on your growth, not collecting mentors. Be intentional about the time frame in which you invite new mentors to join your journey.

1. Industry expert mentor;
2. Fundraising and investment mentor;
3. Efficiency and leadership mentor;
4. Financial mentor;
5. Peer mentor;
6. Technical or product mentor;
7. Brand and marketing mentor; and
8. Personal development mentor.

Building a network of mentors takes time, but the investment is well worth it. By the end of this chapter, you'll have a clear understanding of what type of mentors to look for during the early days of creating your company and how to make the most out of those mentorship relationships.

Harnessing the Collective Wisdom: Working with Your Network of Mentors

The composition of your mentor network is instrumental in your growth and success. The stage of entrepreneurship you're in will determine the kind of mentors you need and the nature of your interactions with them.

While it may be tempting to gather every type of mentor immediately, this approach can be counterproductive in the long term. Staying focused and seeking mentors only when you have the capacity to do so is important. Managing more than three mentors at once can be overwhelming, preventing you from fully benefiting from your current mentor relationships.

> *The composition of your mentor network is instrumental in your growth and success. The stage of entrepreneurship you're in will determine the kind of mentors you need and the nature of your interactions with them.*

The Industry Expert Mentor

An industry mentor is someone who possesses extensive experience and knowledge within your business's specific industry and can offer guidance on market trends, sales cycles, regulations, and other industry-specific issues and nuances. Their insights are invaluable for early-stage entrepreneurs seeking to navigate the complexities of their chosen field.

Role and Characteristics

The industry mentor offers specialized expertise that extends beyond general business advice. They have a deep understanding of market dynamics, customer behaviors, and competitive forces. Their guidance is practical, strategic, and tailored to the unique challenges faced by entrepreneurs within the industry.

The industry mentor acts as a subject matter expert, guiding entrepreneurs in understanding customer needs, identifying untapped opportunities, and developing strategies that resonate within the industry.

Example

Consider Maya, an early-stage entrepreneur launching a business in the renewable energy sector. She connects with Autumn, an entrepreneur industry mentor with decades of experience in renewable energy.

Autumn helps Maya navigate the regulatory landscape, ensuring she understands permits and compliance requirements. She also shares insights about emerging technologies and market trends, positioning Maya's business for future growth. Autumn's mentorship is pivotal, enabling Maya to make informed decisions aligned with industry best practices.

Pros	Cons
In-depth insights: This mentor provides insights into industry-specific challenges, enabling entrepreneurs to make informed decisions.	Limited perspective: Industry mentors may have a narrower focus, potentially overlooking insights from other sectors that could drive innovation.
Market intelligence: They share valuable knowledge about historical data and trends, allowing entrepreneurs to stay ahead of the curve and seize emerging opportunities.	Changing landscape: Industry dynamics can shift rapidly, and outdated advice from the mentor may not align with evolving trends.
Regulatory guidance: The mentor helps entrepreneurs navigate complex regulations, avoiding potential pitfalls and legal hurdles.	Risk of industry bias: Mentors deeply embedded in an industry may have biases or affiliations that influence their guidance, limiting objectivity.
Network access: Entrepreneurs gain access to the mentor's industry network, opening doors to potential collaborators, customers, and partners.	Competition concerns: Be cautious when sharing proprietary information with mentors who operate within the same industry.
Strategic positioning: This mentor assists entrepreneurs in strategically positioning their offerings to stand out within the industry.	

Sample Questions to Ask

- How can I stay updated with the latest trends in our industry to remain competitive in the market?
- Could you provide an example of how your expertise helped a company at this stage overcome a major challenge and the lessons learned from that experience?

- What factors distinguish successful businesses in our industry from those that struggle?
- How should I identify and target our ideal customer segment given consumer behaviors in our industry?
- What strategies have you seen work for building partnerships and collaborations within the industry that could benefit early-stage businesses like mine?

The Fundraising and Investment Mentor

A fundraising and investment mentor is an expert in securing capital and navigating the complexities of fundraising. They guide start-ups in creating effective pitch decks and connecting with potential investors.

Role and Characteristics

The fundraising and investment mentor has extensive experience in fundraising, with a deep understanding of what it takes to secure capital. They might be an investor themselves or have a history of assisting businesses in their fundraising efforts.

Example

Consider Marcus, an early-stage entrepreneur who is launching an innovative health care company. Marcus connects with Sophia, a fundraising and investment mentor who has a track record of successfully securing funding for early-stage businesses in the health and wellness sector. Sophia helps Marcus refine his pitch deck, highlighting key benefits and the unique value proposition of his product that she knows investors will want to know. Once he's ready to present, she introduces Marcus to a network of investors who have a keen interest in health care–related innovations. With Sophia's guidance, Marcus navigates investor meetings and secures the funding needed to bring his vision to life.

The fundraising and investment mentor's role extends beyond funding advice. They provide insights into investor expectations, negotiation tactics, and strategies for maintaining post-funding investor relations.

Pros	Cons
Extensive network: Fundraising and investment mentors have a network of potential investors, increasing their chances of finding suitable funding sources for your business.	Narrow focus: Fundraising and investment mentors may primarily focus on fundraising aspects, potentially overlooking other critical business areas.
Fundraising strategy: The mentor helps entrepreneurs create a strategic fundraising plan, including target funding amounts, valuation considerations, and timeline projections.	Changing investor landscape: As investor preferences evolve, advice from the mentor may become outdated if not aligned with current trends.
Negotiation expertise: This mentor equips entrepreneurs with negotiation skills to navigate terms, valuations, and investment agreements effectively.	Limited scope: The mentor's expertise may not cover broader business strategy areas beyond fundraising, such as product development or market positioning.
	Risk of overemphasis: Overemphasis on fundraising may lead to a narrow perspective, neglecting the importance of building a robust business model.

Sample Questions to Ask

- How should I tailor my pitch deck for different types of investors, such as angel investors versus venture capitalists?
- What common mistakes do entrepreneurs make during investor meetings, and how can I avoid them?
- What strategies work best for building relationships with potential investors?
- When should I start fundraising, and do I need to pursue venture capital or continue bootstrapping?
- How should I structure my cap table? What happens if I continue bootstrapping instead?
- I'm having difficulty fine-tuning the go-to-market strategy and funding allocation sections of my investor pitch. Could you provide feedback on its clarity and suggest how to make it more concise?

The Efficiency and Leadership Mentor

An efficiency and leadership mentor helps you optimize your business operations, streamline processes, and cultivate effective leadership skills. This mentor brings a wealth of experience in running and scaling businesses, offering invaluable insights into operations, logistics, and growth strategies. This is a mentor who can help you develop critical leadership skills, build a high-performing team, and navigate the challenges of being a founder and CEO.

Role and Characteristics

The efficiency and leadership mentor is well versed in the intricacies of business operations and growth strategies. With a proven track record of successfully scaling ventures, they offer guidance on operational efficiency, resource allocation, and innovative tactics to accelerate growth. This mentor is a trusted advisor who helps entrepreneurs navigate the challenges of leadership and provides actionable insights to build high-performing teams.

The efficiency and leadership mentor is also adept at helping entrepreneurs navigate the challenges of leadership, team management, and sustaining growth momentum.

Pros	Cons
Optimized operations: Entrepreneurs gain insights into improving processes, enhancing resource allocation, and reducing inefficiencies.	Niche expertise: The mentor's focus on operations and leadership may not cover all aspects of entrepreneurship, potentially overlooking specialized areas.
Growth hacking: This mentor offers strategies to accelerate growth, leveraging innovative approaches to expand market reach.	Changing business landscape: Strategies for efficiency and growth can vary based on market trends, and outdated advice may not be as effective.

(Continued)

Pros	Cons
Leadership development: Entrepreneurs receive guidance on honing leadership skills, building high-performing teams, and nurturing a culture of innovation.	Overemphasis on scaling: Prioritizing growth without considering operational readiness can lead to challenges in managing expansion.
Problem solving: The mentor's experience equips entrepreneurs with problem-solving techniques to address challenges and seize opportunities.	
Sustainable scaling: Mentors provide insights into scaling strategies that ensure growth is manageable and aligned with the business's capacity.	

Sample Questions to Ask

- How can I identify operational bottlenecks and inefficiencies in my business, and what strategies can I implement to address them?
- What steps can I take to develop a scalable growth strategy that aligns with my business's strengths and market opportunities?
- Could you share a specific instance where your expertise in operations and leadership led to significant improvements in a company's performance?
- What approaches do you recommend for building and leading a high-performing team that is aligned with the company's vision and goals?
- As an entrepreneur, how can I strike a balance between hands-on involvement in operations and delegating tasks effectively to my team?

Financial Mentor

A financial mentor is vital for early-stage entrepreneurs tackling the intricacies of business finance, funding, and fiscal decisions. With their extensive knowledge in financial management, they offer bespoke advice to address the distinctive fiscal challenges and objectives of early-stage businesses. Distinct from a fundraising and investment mentor, their role centers on improving the broader financial well-being of both the founder and the business, beyond just venture capital and fundraising activities.

Role and Characteristics

A financial mentor has expertise in financial planning, management, and analysis. They bring knowledge in budgeting, cash flow management, fundraising, and investment strategies, acting as a trusted advisor to help entrepreneurs make informed financial decisions that support business growth and sustainability.

Example

Leo runs a rapidly expanding vegan bakery but struggled with forecasting, budgeting, and financial projections. Seeking expertise, they connected with Brenda, a financial mentor experienced in small business finances. Brenda helped Leo devise a comprehensive financial plan, including realistic budgeting and projections, tailored to their bakery's growth trajectory. She also guided them in identifying suitable investment opportunities. With Brenda's insights and support, Leo successfully secured the necessary investment, positioning their bakery to effectively meet the surging demand.

The financial mentor's expertise extends beyond day-to-day financial matters, enabling entrepreneurs to make informed financial decisions that drive their business's success.

Pros	Cons
Financial literacy: Entrepreneurs gain a fundamental understanding of financial concepts and best practices, empowering them to make informed decisions.	Industry relevance: The mentor's financial expertise may not be tailored to the specific industry nuances of the entrepreneur's business.

(Continued)

Pros	Cons
Budgeting and cash flow management: Mentors offer guidance on creating budgets, managing expenses, and optimizing cash flow to ensure financial stability.	Changing financial landscape: The financial landscape can evolve rapidly, and the mentor's strategies may not always align with current market conditions.
Funding strategies: Entrepreneurs receive insights into various funding options, including venture capital, angel investment, and bootstrapping.	Risk tolerance: The mentor's risk tolerance may differ from that of the entrepreneur, potentially influencing financial decisions.
Investment planning: The mentor provides advice on investment strategies to grow surplus funds and generate returns.	Limited focus: The mentor's advice may primarily focus on financial matters, potentially overlooking other aspects of entrepreneurship.
Risk mitigation: Entrepreneurs learn how to identify and manage financial risks, ensuring resilience in the face of economic challenges.	

Sample Questions to Ask

- How can I create a realistic financial plan that aligns with my business goals and growth projections?
- What funding options are suitable for my business, and how should I approach securing investment?
- Could you provide guidance on effective cash flow management to maintain financial stability?
- What key financial metrics should I regularly monitor to assess my business's health?
- How can I balance investing in business growth with maintaining personal financial stability?

Peer Mentor

A peer mentor for early-stage entrepreneurs plays a pivotal role in providing relatable guidance, shared experiences, and valuable insights.

This mentor is someone who has walked a similar path, who has a business that is two to three years ahead of your current business maturity, and can offer support and understanding based on their own entrepreneurial journey. They do not need to be in your same industry, but they have a deep understanding of what it takes to build a business at your current stage with relevant resources, tools, and advice to mitigate immediate business concerns.

Role and Characteristics

A peer mentor brings an insightful perspective, having navigated the complexities and opportunities of entrepreneurship themselves. They have direct knowledge of the ups and downs faced in the early stages of a business and are equipped to offer practical advice and empathetic support. Their counsel is based on real-world experiences, making it particularly pertinent and actionable.

Example

Maya has recently launched an innovative financial empowerment platform. She connected with Alex, a peer mentor who had successfully founded a similar platform years prior. Alex had a wealth of experience dealing with market entry, user acquisition, and forming strategic partnerships. As a peer mentor, Alex offered Maya valuable advice on scaling her platform, improving user experience, and navigating regulatory hurdles. Their mentorship helped accelerate the growth of Maya's financial empowerment tech platform.

A peer mentor acts as an empathetic confidant, providing support during challenging times and celebrating successes together. They foster camaraderie and a sense of community, encouraging open conversations about hurdles, goals, and aspirations. This mentorship dynamic promotes shared growth and a strong sense of community among entrepreneurs.

Pros	Cons
Relevance: Peer mentors offer advice tailored to current entrepreneurial trends and challenges, providing insights that resonate with your journey.	Limited expertise: Peer mentors may have specialized knowledge in certain areas, potentially overlooking broader aspects of entrepreneurship.
Realistic expectations: They provide a realistic view of the entrepreneurial path, helping you set achievable goals and manage expectations.	Varied paths: Each entrepreneur's journey is unique, and solutions that worked for one mentee may not apply to another's specific context.
Network expansion: Peer mentors often introduce you to their own network, opening doors to potential collaborations, partnerships, and customers.	Time constraints: Peer mentors may have limited availability due to their own business responsibilities, affecting the frequency of interactions.
Motivation and empowerment: Seeing another entrepreneur's success story can motivate and empower you, instilling confidence and determination.	
Adaptive learning: Peer mentors adjust their advice based on the latest trends and changes, ensuring you stay agile in your approach.	

Sample Questions to Ask

- Could you share a challenge you faced early on and how you overcame it?
- How did you build your first prototype and cost-effectively test hypotheses?
- What strategies did you use for user acquisition and customer engagement?
- How do you ensure mental well-being while building a company?
- How do you stay adaptable to industry trends while focusing on your start-up's core goals?
- What strategies have you used to build a strong, engaged community around your product or service?

The Technical or Product Mentor

A technical or product mentor, skilled in specific technologies or essential business skills, helps clarify technical and product-related complexities. They are knowledgeable in areas like manufacturing, inventory management, product fulfillment, packaging, and shipping. In the context of a technology company, they bring expertise in software development, data analysis, or engineering, playing a significant role in your product's success.

Role and Characteristics

This mentor bridges the knowledge gap for entrepreneurs eager to harness technology for their business growth. They have a thorough understanding of relevant tools, methodologies, and industry standards, positioning them to offer tailored guidance for the technical challenges and opportunities faced by entrepreneurs.

Example

Rahul is developing an AI-driven e-commerce platform and connects with Sara, a mentor known for her machine learning and artificial intelligence proficiency. Under Sara's guidance, Rahul gains insights into algorithm selection, data preprocessing, and model optimization. Sara provides actionable advice for incorporating AI into the platform, enhancing user experience, and utilizing predictive analytics for customer engagement. Sara's technical acumen and practical advice enrich Rahul's product development journey.

Example

Carla is launching a vegan ice cream business and seeks mentorship from Derrick, renowned for his expertise in order fulfillment and product preservation. Under Derrick's mentorship, Carla learns innovative techniques for extending her ice cream's freshness and shelf life. Derrick advises on efficient order processing, maintaining product quality during shipping, and utilizing eco-friendly packaging solutions. His expertise in logistics and refrigeration systems saves Carla over $800 per month in inventory waste. Derrick's strategic guidance and practical solutions significantly enhance Carla's ability to deliver a superior, long-lasting vegan ice cream product to her customers, bolstering her business's success.

These mentors are adept at translating complex technical concepts into understandable insights, enabling mentees to make well-informed decisions and create products that resonate with their audience.

Pros	Cons
Specialized expertise: Mentors provide targeted guidance on technological challenges, ensuring product development is informed by best practices.	Niche focus: These mentors may have a specialized skill set, potentially limiting their guidance to technical and product-related areas.
Accelerated learning: Mentees gain insights into the latest technologies and tools, allowing them to stay ahead of industry trends.	Technical jargon: Communicating technical concepts to nontechnical team members may require additional effort to ensure clear understanding.
Quality assurance: Technical or product mentors help in quality control, ensuring that products meet technical standards and user expectations.	Evolution of technology: Rapid technological advancements may render some insights outdated over time.
Innovative solutions: They encourage innovative thinking, helping entrepreneurs explore unconventional approaches to product development.	
Problem solving: Mentors assist in troubleshooting technical issues, helping mentees overcome hurdles efficiently.	

Sample Questions to Ask

- What should I consider when choosing technologies for my product development, given the current tech landscape?
- How can I build a scalable architecture for my software product to accommodate future growth?

- What is your approach to data analysis and interpretation for product improvement?
- Could you share a technical challenge you faced during your product development and its resolution?
- What strategies can I use to clearly convey technical concepts to nontechnical stakeholders such as investors or customers?
- I want our brand to project professionalism. How can we develop cost-effective, sustainable packaging while utilizing customer feedback to enhance our product?

The Brand and Marketing Mentor

A brand or marketing mentor is a vital guide for early-stage entrepreneurs striving to develop a solid brand presence and successfully market their products or services. This mentor has knowledge in crafting brand strategies, creating detailed marketing plans, and running successful campaigns that connect with target audiences while also establishing your executive presence.

Role and Characteristics

The brand and marketing mentor is essential in helping an entrepreneur shape their approach to branding and marketing. They have a comprehensive understanding of consumer behavior, market trends, and effective communication strategies, providing the entrepreneur with important insights for building compelling brand narratives and engaging customers successfully.

Example

Claire is introducing an innovative line of sustainable fashion accessories and seeks guidance from Abbey, an experienced brand and marketing mentor with a successful history in brand campaigns. Abbey assists Claire in identifying her brand's core values, positioning, and unique selling points. Together, they develop a detailed marketing plan that incorporates social media engagement, influencer partnerships, and interactive campaigns. Through Abbey's expertise, Claire is equipped to introduce a brand that appeals to eco-conscious consumers and stands out in the market.

A brand and marketing mentor serves as a trusted advisor, offering strategic insights to entrepreneurs looking to establish a compelling brand narrative and engage customers through effective marketing strategies.

Pros	Cons
Strategic branding: They guide entrepreneurs in developing a brand strategy that aligns with their vision, values, and target audience.	Industry specificity: Brand builders/ marketing mentors may have expertise in specific industries, limiting their applicability across diverse sectors.
Comprehensive marketing plans: Mentors assist in crafting detailed marketing plans encompassing various channels and tactics.	Changing trends: Rapidly evolving marketing trends and platforms require mentors to stay up-to-date to offer relevant advice.
Effective campaigns: They offer insights into campaign planning, content creation, and distribution strategies to maximize reach and impact.	Time commitment: Entrepreneurs must ensure a reasonable time commitment from mentors, as intensive campaign development may demand more resources.
Storytelling expertise: Brand builders excel in creating compelling brand narratives that resonate with customers on an emotional level.	Creative subjectivity: Recommendations for branding and marketing strategies may be influenced by personal creative preferences, which may not align with the entrepreneur's vision.
Market differentiation: Brand builders help entrepreneurs differentiate their offerings in competitive markets through unique positioning.	
Customer engagement: Mentors provide guidance on fostering meaningful customer relationships through authentic brand interactions.	
Brand consistency: They ensure consistency across all brand touchpoints, building trust and recognition among consumers.	

Sample Questions to Ask

- How can I concisely explain my company to evoke excitement from my customers, ideally in 30 seconds or less?
- What is your process for developing a brand strategy that resonates with a target audience's values and preferences?
- Could you provide examples of successful marketing campaigns you've managed and the strategies that made them effective?
- How do you determine the most suitable marketing channels for a specific product or service?
- What recommendations do you have for maintaining brand consistency across various marketing touchpoints?
- How do you evaluate the success of a marketing campaign and adjust strategies based on performance metrics?
- If you had a budget of $500 for social media marketing, how would you allocate that money?

Personal Development Mentor

The personal development mentor is essential in helping early-stage entrepreneurs develop a growth-oriented mindset, boost their personal effectiveness, and tackle the hurdles of entrepreneurship with resilience and clarity. This mentor supports your personal and professional growth, offering advice on time management, productivity, maintaining a meaningful social life, and setting achievable goals.

Role and Characteristics

The personal development mentor prioritizes holistic growth by addressing key areas that significantly affect an entrepreneur's success. They provide insights, strategies, and tools to enhance time management, boost productivity, establish meaningful goals, and focus on self-well-being. By sharing knowledge and techniques related to personal development, this mentor equips entrepreneurs to overcome obstacles, handle stress, and achieve a healthy work-life balance.

Example

Consider the example of Rupa, an early-stage entrepreneur eager to launch an online fitness platform. Rupa collaborates with Chris, a mentor experienced in personal development and known for successfully running a fitness business while maintaining a balanced lifestyle that prioritizes time to attend his children's soccer games and time to rest on weekends. Chris guides Rupa in setting achievable goals, effectively balancing business responsibilities with personal pursuits, and adopting self-care practices to prevent burnout. Through Chris's mentorship, Rupa gains critical insights, enabling her to skillfully navigate the entrepreneurial journey while prioritizing her well-being.

Pros	Cons
Time management mastery: Entrepreneurs learn techniques to manage their time efficiently, allocate resources effectively, and avoid feeling overwhelmed.	Subjectivity: Recommendations related to personal development may be influenced by the mentor's personal experiences and preferences, which may not align with all mentee's needs.
Self-reflection: Personal development mentors encourage self-awareness, self-discovery, and continuous self-improvement.	Lack of business focus: Personal development mentors may prioritize personal growth over business-specific strategies, potentially overlooking key aspects of entrepreneurship such as marketing, sales, or operations.
Goal-setting expertise: Entrepreneurs gain insights into setting goals that align with their vision, creating a road map for success.	
Stress management: Personal development mentors offer tools to manage stress, maintain focus, and cultivate a resilient mindset.	
Work-life integration: They guide entrepreneurs in achieving a healthy work-life balance, preventing burnout and fostering well-being.	

Sample Questions to Ask

- What are your recommendations for balancing entrepreneurial demands with personal well-being to avert burnout?
- Could you detail time management and priority-setting techniques to enhance productivity?
- How have you addressed family discussions about choosing entrepreneurship over a stable nine-to-five job?
- Would you mind sharing methods for establishing and monitoring meaningful goals?
- Which strategies do you find effective for stress management and sustaining a growth mindset amid difficulties?
- How do you incorporate self-care into your daily routine for a balanced entrepreneurial life?
- Is there a leadership coach you endorse?
- What are your tips for task prioritization and time management to prevent feeling swamped?
- How do you suggest maintaining a work-life balance while undertaking entrepreneurial responsibilities?
- In facing challenges and setbacks, how do you preserve a positive and resilient mindset?
- How might I foster self-motivation and a mindset oriented toward growth for success?

Elevator Overview

In previous chapters, we emphasized the significance of making a memorable first impression with potential mentors. When engaging with prospective mentors for yourself or your business, prioritize brevity and aim to spark deeper dialogue. This isn't the occasion to present your entire business plan or seek funding, but rather to introduce yourself and engage in an open conversation. Here are three examples of succinct 30–45 second pitches tailored for interactions with new acquaintances and potential mentors.

Why This Matters

In the dynamic environment of entrepreneurship, where time is a valuable commodity, a well-crafted elevator pitch shows respect for the mentor's time.

In the dynamic environment of entrepreneurship, where time is a valuable commodity, a well-crafted elevator pitch shows respect for the mentor's time. It conveys your message succinctly, creating a strong foundation for future dialogues. Furthermore, a personalized pitch displays your genuine interest in the mentor's wisdom, increasing the chances of a continued interaction.

A confident delivery of your elevator pitch can enhance your self-assurance when engaging with potential mentors. This positive demeanor can shape the mentor's impression of your competence in tackling challenges. Moreover, a well-rehearsed pitch showcases your professionalism and commitment, reflecting your dedication to your business and the mentoring process.

At events where you may meet various individuals, your elevator pitch is an efficient way to introduce yourself and your business succinctly, potentially leading to more expansive dialogues if the mentor is intrigued. This opens doors to deeper discussions about your ambitions and obstacles.

In essence, a well-developed elevator pitch is an essential instrument for entrepreneurs in pursuit of mentorship. It encapsulates the essence of your business and your background, allowing mentors to quickly grasp the nature of your enterprise. By leaving a lasting impression and creating opportunities for substantive discussions, your elevator pitch can significantly influence your mentorship experiences and propel your entrepreneurial journey forward.

Example: Pottery Business

I'm an enthusiastic potter who has transformed my passion for ceramics into a thriving business, Artisan Earthware. My artistic background has equipped me with the skills necessary to craft unique, handmade pottery items that merge traditional methods with contemporary design. My objective is to unite art with practicality. At present, I'm in search of a mentor to help me expand my pottery business while preserving the unique qualities and craftsmanship that distinguish my work.

Example: PR Company

I recently started a PR agency dedicated to enhancing the presence of brands with meaningful missions. My background in PR equips me to assist businesses in creating a significant impact and flourishing in our modern media environment. Presently, I am fine-tuning approaches to increase my online presence and foster community connections. I am seeking a mentor who can provide wisdom on developing a solid client base and successfully adapting to the changing digital PR landscape.

Example: Sustainable Tech Company

I'm Chris, the cofounder of GreenTech Innovators. Our start-up is on a mission to modernize the 3D printed home construction industry with sustainable materials. With a background in engineering, I've always been passionate about finding eco-friendly solutions. Our team is developing cutting-edge products that reduce environmental impact. I'm eager to connect with a mentor who has experience in scaling tech companies and navigating the sustainability sector.

Making the Ask

Securing a mentor as an entrepreneur involves a strategic approach to making the ask. This pivotal step isn't just about identifying a suitable mentor; it's also about reaching out to them in a manner that resonates with their values while aligning with your business goals.

The approach to inviting someone to be your mentor involves a brief conversation, facilitated by the components in the following sections. This approach is valuable for all early interactions with potential mentors and offers a template that guides the potential mentor through your mindset, intentions, and objectives. Crafting a clear and concise ask makes it easier to prompt a positive or negative response, allowing you to move forward accordingly.

> *Before reaching out to a potential mentor, be sure to take a moment to reflect on your motivations. Consider the qualities and attributes that make this individual a potential mentor, and reflect on the alignment between their journey and your aspirations.*

Before reaching out to a potential mentor, be sure to take a moment to reflect on your motivations. Consider the qualities and attributes that make this individual a potential mentor, and reflect on the alignment between their journey and your aspirations. This reflective exercise establishes a common ground and demonstrates your thoughtful approach to mentorship. I encourage you to read Chapter 7 for more guidance on how to prepare to invite someone to join you as your mentor.

Crafting the Initial Contact Message

After considering what you desire in a mentor, it's time to compose an email to propose a potential mentorship. Write concisely and professionally, focusing on arranging a meeting to discuss the possibility of working together. Highlight your admiration for their achievements and explain how their experience resonates with your professional aspirations. Maintain a tone of professionalism and appreciation throughout your correspondence.

Here Is a Template for Your Outreach Email

Subject: Exploring a mentorship opportunity
Hello [Mentor's name],

Your professional path and achievements, particularly in [specific area], have greatly inspired me. I believe your insights could be instrumental in shaping my entrepreneurial journey.

I am reaching out to see if you would be interested in a mentorship connection. Your expertise in [specific areas] is precisely aligned with my entrepreneurial aspirations, and I am keen to learn from someone of your caliber.

Could we arrange a short call or meeting at your earliest convenience to see if there's a potential for a mentoring relationship?

I am confident that your mentorship could be significantly beneficial as I progress in the business world.

Thank you for considering my request. I am enthusiastic about the prospect of connecting with you.

Best regards,

[Your name]

Taking the time to structure your approach when making the ask can significantly improve the outcome. By acknowledging the shared experience and creating a personal connection, you show that your request is genuine and well-considered. Crafting a thoughtful outreach email conveys your seriousness about mentorship while respecting the potential mentor's time and expertise.

How to Structure Your Mentor Invitation Meeting

When the potential mentor responds positively to your outreach, it's time to arrange a meeting to discuss the possibility of mentorship further. There are six steps to follow.

Align Goals and Availability

Begin the conversation by sharing why you admire their journey and expertise. Personalize your approach to reflect your genuine interest in their contributions. Keep your points succinct and focused, highlighting their relevant skills and strengths that align with your goals.

Define Mutual Objectives and Clarify Your Goals

During your discussion, clearly express your goals and what you hope to gain from the mentorship. Communicate the specific value you anticipate their advice will bring, whether that's sharpening certain skills, acquiring insights, or navigating your business journey. Make sure your potential mentor understands the mutual benefits of their guidance. Outlining your objectives shows your dedication to a productive mentoring relationship.

Share Your Proposed Mentorship Timeline

When discussing the mentorship, be open about the time commitment you're seeking. Propose a realistic frequency of interactions, whether it's monthly meetings, biweekly check-ins, or occasional conversations. Your respect for their time and proactive approach will be appreciated. Flexibility is key, and be ready to adjust the schedule to accommodate their availability.

Discuss Milestones and Phases

Offer a detailed plan of the mentorship's progression, sectioned into distinct phases, each with specific milestones and goals. Presenting this organized approach will show your potential mentor your initiative and commitment. It's a chance to specify the steps you plan to take and confirm that you and your mentor have a shared understanding of the path ahead.

Seek Feedback to Refine Your Approach

Throughout the conversation, encourage feedback and seek alignment. This demonstrates your willingness to adapt and optimize the mentorship engagement. Ensure that your approach resonates with them and clarifies expectations on both sides. By confirming mutual understanding, you're establishing a strong foundation for a successful mentorship relationship.

Example Script

I've closely followed your career and am deeply impressed by your successes in [mentor's specific field]. Your skills and experience stand out, and your commitment to [pull something this person has said in a previous conversation] inspires me.

I'm at the beginning stages of founding my company and would greatly benefit from your guidance. Your talent for [specific achievement or skill, e.g. crafting successful product-market fit strategies] aligns with the challenges I'm currently facing.

I hope to invite you to be my mentor. With your insights, I'll focus on integrating my product into our target customers' lives and identify key customer relationships. My vision includes monthly one-hour meetings, where I'd value your insights on my product strategy, product-market fit, and audience connection. Your expertise in [relevant area, e.g. analyzing consumer behavior] would be invaluable.

I deeply respect your work and its industry impact. To have you as a mentor would be extraordinary. Could we discuss this further? What are your thoughts?

The process of making the ask involves strategic thinking, clear communication, and a genuine connection. Crafting a powerful outreach email, aligning goals, setting expectations, and charting a mentorship path will help you secure a mentor who aligns with your entrepreneurial aspirations. Approach the process with respect for their time, an eagerness to learn, and a commitment to making the mentorship relationship a mutually beneficial one.

11A

Full Circle: Embracing the Next Phase of Your Mentorship Journey

As WE WRAP up our chapters on securing mentors and evolving into an effective mentee, bear in mind that this process is not static. There is no one-size-fits-all answer, and you have the liberty to try out different methods within the options presented in this book. Patience will be your greatest companion as you tread this path, and making mindful choices is pivotal as the mentor relationships you form will significantly influence your career.

Statistics show that 89% of individuals who have been mentored will, in turn, mentor others.[1] The forthcoming two chapters will prime you for this transition from mentee to mentor. Much like your pursuit of guidance and support, you will soon find yourself in the position to bestow these invaluable insights on others. This transformation requires a comprehensive grasp of your duties as a mentor, and the ensuing chapters will furnish you with the requisite know-how to flourish in this role.

Remember, mentorship is reciprocal. These upcoming chapters will also serve as a beneficial guide for your mentors, ensuring everyone is united in cultivating sustainable, meaningful mentorship relationships. By exploring the characteristics of an ideal mentor through their lens, you will acquire the essential tools to discern if someone is a suitable match for your mentoring trajectory. Stay dedicated, stay attentive, and don't forget that your career warrants nothing short of your best effort.

12

Core Principles for Becoming
an Effective Mentor

As MY TEAM and I helped notable companies build mentorship programs through The Mentor Method, a surprising discovery unfolded as I met with mentors eager to understand the nuances of effective mentorship. This curiosity intrigued me, given that these mentors had been hand-picked by their employers, recognized for their unique skills, and celebrated as exemplifying the organization's desired qualities in future talent. However, a significant gap seemed to exist between their selection and their perceptions of what it takes to make a genuine impact as mentors.

As I explored this further, I found a consistent pattern emerging. We invest significant effort in preparing mentees on how to find and connect with mentors, but we often overlook the equally important step of ensuring that mentors themselves feel confident and adequately equipped for their role in the mentorship relationship.

My personal journey from being a mentee to becoming a mentor was marked by a similar sense of uncertainty.

> *We invest significant effort in preparing mentees on how to find and connect with mentors, but we often overlook the equally important step of ensuring that mentors themselves feel confident and adequately equipped for their role in the mentorship relationship.*

After The Mentor Method's acquisition, I felt a strong responsibility to share my entrepreneurial knowledge and help fellow entrepreneurs achieve success more efficiently. However, even with my accolades, recognition, and extensive lived experiences that I had internalized, I found myself grappling with uncertainty. I questioned whether my experiences were adequate or beneficial to others and had to confront the self-doubt in my mind that told me I might not be adequately prepared to mentor others.

Through guidance from my mentors, evaluating my own capacity to mentor, a comprehensive understanding of what effective mentorship entails, and ensuring that I adhered to the guiding principles outlined in this chapter, I gradually learned how to be an effective mentor that aligned with the self-discovery work outlined in Chapter 2. The results have been profoundly rewarding. There's nothing quite like the feeling of seeing your mentees succeed in a pitch competition, build their teams with skill, or address critical business challenges with ease, often in just a month, compared to the eight months it took me to navigate similar issues. All of this emphasizes that mentorship can be demanding; we're not always explicitly taught how to excel in this role, but I firmly believe that if I could learn to do it effectively, you can too. In the upcoming two chapters, we'll embark on this journey together and continue growing as mentors.

The role of a mentor is a distinguished honor, but it can also carry immense pressure, particularly if you are new to this role. The moment you're recognized as an expert, be it officially or informally, your mentee's expectations can weigh heavily on your shoulders. While there is a wealth of information on how to excel as a mentee or establish meaningful mentorship relationships (as demonstrated in this book), it's imperative that you, as a mentor, feel empowered and well prepared to fulfill your role. This chapter and the next serve as a mentor's foundational guide, offering an all-encompassing view of what it means to be an effective mentor and helping you embrace this new chapter in your professional journey.

Defining Mentorship through Your Lens as a Mentor

As you reflect on your own career journey, take a moment to acknowledge the mentors who played pivotal roles in your professional development.

These were the individuals who offered guidance, provided valuable advice, and offered constructive feedback that helped steer your path toward success. Now, envision extending this positive influence to the lives of others, empowering them to realize their potential and achieve success. This is what mentorship represents.

Those who choose to be mentors often benefit as well. Research shows that 57% of mentors expand their skill sets, compared to 40% of non-mentors. Additionally, 43% deepen their understanding of their customer base, versus 26% of non-mentors, and 30% enhance their knowledge of potential new customers or market segments, compared to 19% among non-mentors.

Mentorship is a two-way relationship in which both parties benefit; it also provides an opportunity to transition from being a mentee to a mentor at different stages of your career. A significant 89% of individuals who have received mentoring themselves proceed to mentor others in their professional journeys. If you, like the 92% of senior executives who credit their success to mentors, are eager to explore the realm of mentorship, then you've come to the right place.

Behavioral Indicators of a Successful and Unsuccessful Mentor

After examining numerous mentorship relationships and exploring what contributes to their success or shortcomings, I noticed frequent patterns and identified a set of behavioral attributes that can serve as valuable indicators of a mentor's effectiveness. When I refer to "successful" or "unsuccessful" mentors, I'm referring to the impact these relationships have on both the mentee's career and the overall satisfaction of both parties involved. Here's a breakdown of these behavioral attributes for you to consider. This list serves as a guide to help you identify your strengths and areas where you might focus on improvement.

When I refer to "successful" or "unsuccessful" mentors, I'm referring to the impact these relationships have on both the mentee's career and the overall satisfaction of both parties involved.

Behavioral Indicators of a Successful Mentor:

Active listening and empathy: A successful mentor demonstrates genuine interest in their mentee's experiences, challenges, and aspirations. They actively listen, ask probing questions, and show empathy to understand the mentee's perspective and feelings.

Open communication: Effective mentors maintain open lines of communication, encouraging honest and transparent discussions. They create a safe space for mentees to share their thoughts, concerns, and achievements without fear of judgment.

Guidance and constructive feedback: A successful mentor provides guidance and practical advice based on their own experiences. They offer constructive feedback that helps the mentee identify areas for improvement while highlighting their strengths.

Goal-oriented approach: Mentors with a positive impact assist their mentees in setting clear goals and defining actionable steps to achieve them. They hold mentees accountable and support them in tracking their progress.

Availability and accessibility: A successful mentor makes themselves available for regular meetings and interactions. They respond promptly to messages and demonstrate a willingness to invest time and effort in the mentorship relationship.

Willingness to share knowledge: Effective mentors freely share their knowledge, insights, and industry expertise. They offer resources, recommend relevant books or articles, and provide exposure to new ideas and perspectives.

Championing growth: A successful mentor advocates for their mentee's growth and development. They challenge mentees to step out of their comfort zones, take calculated risks, and embrace opportunities for learning and advancement.

Networking and connections: Mentors with a positive impact leverage their network to connect mentees with relevant professionals, potential collaborators, or opportunities for career advancement.

Long-term perspective: Effective mentors focus on the mentee's long-term development rather than immediate results. They encourage continuous learning, adaptability, and a mindset of resilience in the face of challenges.

Celebrating success: A successful mentor celebrates the mentee's achievements and milestones. They take pride in their mentee's progress and provide encouragement and recognition for their hard work.

Flexibility and adaptability: Mentors with a positive impact are flexible in their approach, adapting their guidance and support based on the mentee's evolving needs and circumstances.

Integrity: Effective mentors lead by example, demonstrating professionalism, ethical behavior, and integrity in their actions. They serve as role models, showcasing values that inspire their mentees.

Lifelong learning: A successful mentor embodies a commitment to lifelong learning and personal growth. They continually seek new knowledge, skills, and experiences to share with their mentees.

Respect for diversity: Mentors with a positive impact embrace diversity and cultural differences. They respect the unique backgrounds, perspectives, and identities of their mentees.

Encouraging independence: Effective mentors empower mentees to make informed decisions and take ownership of their growth journey. They foster independence and self-reliance while offering guidance when needed.

These behavioral indicators collectively characterize a successful mentor who positively influences and guides their mentees toward achieving their professional and personal goals. By incorporating these into their mentorship approach, mentors can create a positive and powerful experience for their mentees and contribute to their personal and professional growth.

Behavioral Indicators of an Unsuccessful Mentor

It's important to acknowledge that not all mentorship interactions are equally successful. Just as positive mentor traits can elevate a mentee's experience, there are also certain behavioral indicators that signal an unsuccessful mentor.

Lack of engagement: An unsuccessful mentor exhibits disinterest or minimal engagement in interactions with their mentee. They may appear distracted, fail to actively participate in conversations, or provide vague responses.

Unavailability: Ineffective mentors consistently show unavailability for scheduled meetings, reschedule frequently, or do not respond to communication promptly. This behavior can lead to frustration and a lack of progress for the mentee.

Limited feedback: An unsuccessful mentor provides limited or vague feedback to their mentee. They may fail to offer constructive criticism or insights that can aid the mentee's growth and development.

Disregard for goals: Ineffective mentors do not prioritize the mentee's goals or provide guidance that aligns with the mentee's aspirations. They may steer discussions away from relevant topics or not address the mentee's concerns.

Dominating conversations: Unsuccessful mentors dominate conversations, focusing on their own experiences, achievements, or challenges. They may overshadow the mentee's input and fail to actively listen.

Dismissive attitude: An ineffective mentor dismisses the mentee's ideas, concerns, or questions without giving them due consideration. This behavior can discourage open communication and hinder mutual understanding.

Limited networking support: Unsuccessful mentors do not offer assistance in expanding the mentee's network or connecting them with relevant professionals. They may not leverage their connections for the mentee's benefit.

Resistance to change: Ineffective mentors resist adapting their guidance to changing circumstances or new information. They may insist on outdated approaches or advice that does not suit the mentee's needs.

Inconsistent commitment: An unsuccessful mentor displays inconsistent commitment to the mentorship relationship. They may engage sporadically, leaving the mentee uncertain about the mentor's level of involvement.

Lack of empathy: Ineffective mentors lack empathy for the mentee's challenges, struggles, or feelings. They may downplay the mentee's concerns or fail to provide emotional support.

Limited transparency: Unsuccessful mentors are not transparent about their own experiences or challenges. They may withhold relevant information that could benefit the mentee's understanding and growth.

Boundary issues: Unsuccessful mentors may cross professional or personal boundaries, making the mentee uncomfortable. They may share inappropriate information or offer advice that is not relevant to the mentorship.

These behavioral indicators illustrate the qualities of an unsuccessful mentor who fails to provide meaningful guidance, support, and engagement to their mentees. Recognizing these indicators can help you make informed decisions about the mentorship relationships you choose to pursue.

Behavioral Attributes of a Successful Entrepreneur Mentor

Guiding early-stage entrepreneurs on their journey is truly rewarding, and it's worth noting that it comes with its unique set of mentorship needs and opportunities. Entrepreneurs are known for their innovative spirit, willingness to take calculated risks, and an unbridled passion for creating something

Successful entrepreneur mentors possess patience and understand that results take time. They emphasize long-term goals over immediate gains, guiding mentees to build sustainable businesses.

entirely new. To be an effective mentor in this dynamic space, you'll want to embrace some specific behavioral attributes that can empower and assist these emerging business leaders.

Openness to sharing experiences: Successful entrepreneur mentors approach mentorship with a willingness to share their personal experiences. They understand the value of vulnerability, opening up about their triumphs and setbacks. By sharing anecdotes, they provide mentees with relatable examples and practical insights into the challenges and decisions they may encounter.

Example: A mentor might recount a time when their marketing strategy didn't yield the expected results, offering insights into the importance of flexibility and adapting to market feedback.

Patience and long-term perspective: Successful entrepreneur mentors possess patience and understand that results take time. They emphasize long-term goals over immediate gains, guiding mentees to build sustainable businesses. This patient approach is evident when a mentor encourages a mentee to focus on building a strong foundation before pursuing rapid expansion.

Tailored guidance: A hallmark of a successful mentor is their ability to provide personalized guidance. They understand that each mentee's journey is unique and refrain from offering generic solutions. Instead, they consider the mentee's industry, goals, and challenges to provide advice that resonates.

Example: When advising a mentee looking to expand their financial literacy tech platform, the mentor takes into account the platform's target audience and the specific challenges faced within the financial empowerment domain.

Empowerment and challenge: The best mentors empower mentees to make informed decisions and take calculated risks. They inspire mentees to challenge themselves, fostering growth and resilience in the face of adversity.

Example: A mentor encourages a mentee to explore innovative monetization strategies for their platform, pushing them beyond their comfort zone and encouraging creative problem solving.

Constructive feedback: Constructive feedback is a cornerstone of successful mentorship. Effective mentors provide feedback that is actionable and focused on improvement. They highlight both strengths and areas for development, aiding mentees in refining their skills.

Example: While reviewing a business plan, a mentor acknowledges the strong market analysis section and suggests refining the financial projections for greater accuracy.

Behavioral Attributes of an Unsuccessful Entrepreneur Mentor

It's equally important to acknowledge the characteristics that might hinder rather than enhance this journey. Below are the key behavioral traits of entrepreneur mentors that could potentially impede the progress of mentees.

Dominance and dictation: An unsuccessful mentor may assume a dominant role in conversations, offering solutions without seeking input from the mentee. This approach can stifle the mentee's ability to critically analyze situations and make independent decisions.

Example: Instead of considering the mentee's insights, the mentor dictates specific marketing strategies without addressing the unique aspects of the financial empowerment platform.

Dismissal of ideas: Mentors who dismiss or belittle the ideas presented by their mentees discourage open and creative thinking. This can lead to the suppression of innovative concepts and hinder the mentee's confidence in expressing their viewpoints.

Example: The mentor swiftly dismisses the mentee's proposal to collaborate with influencers, failing to recognize its potential for expanding the platform's reach.

One-size-fits-all advice: Ineffective mentors offer generic advice without tailoring it to the mentee's specific context. This lack of personalization can result in solutions that are ill-suited to the mentee's unique business challenges.

Example: The mentor provides advice on scaling the tech platform that doesn't consider the platform's focus on financial empowerment, rendering the guidance ineffective.

Unavailability and lack of commitment: An unsuccessful mentor's unavailability erodes the mentee's trust and confidence in the relationship. Frequent cancellations or rescheduling of meetings without valid reasons convey a lack of commitment, leaving mentees feeling unsupported.

Example: The mentor frequently cancels scheduled mentoring sessions, leaving the mentee frustrated and unsupported during critical phases of their financial empowerment platform's development.

Inflexibility and resistance to change: Mentors who resist change and cling to outdated strategies discourage mentees from exploring innovative approaches, hindering the mentee's growth potential.

Example: The mentor dismisses the mentee's ideas to incorporate digital marketing strategies, insisting on traditional methods despite the tech-savvy audience of the financial empowerment platform.

Disregard for mental and emotional well-being: An unsuccessful mentor may disregard the mentee's mental and emotional well-being, focusing solely on business matters. Ignoring stress and burnout signs can lead to diminished productivity and hinder the mentee's overall success.

Example: Despite the mentee expressing signs of stress and exhaustion, the mentor continues to pressure for immediate results without addressing the mentee's well-being.

In the world of entrepreneurship, the attributes demonstrated by mentors significantly shape the mentees' paths. Choosing a mentor who embodies the qualities of successful mentorship can enhance a mentee's growth, while being aware of the behaviors associated with unsuccessful mentorship is equally important for a fulfilling mentorship experience.

Mentor Do's and Don'ts: Nurturing Effective Mentorship

The role of a mentor carries the responsibility of guiding, empowering, and shaping the professional journey of a mentee. Effective mentorship goes beyond simply sharing knowledge; it involves creating a supportive environment that encourages growth, learning, and mutual respect. Just as there are behaviors and approaches that contribute to successful mentorship, there are also important do's and don'ts that mentors should keep in mind to ensure a meaningful and effective relationship.

Do

Act as a guide and facilitator: A successful mentor recognizes their role as a guide who offers insights and expertise, rather than dictating the path. Facilitate discussions and encourage critical thinking, allowing the mentee to explore possibilities and make informed decisions.

Set clear expectations: Establish clear expectations and goals for the mentorship relationship from the outset. Define the scope of your role, the frequency of interactions, and the objectives you aim to achieve together.

Listen actively: Effective communication starts with active listening. Pay close attention to your mentee's goals, challenges, and aspirations. Encourage them to share their thoughts openly, and provide thoughtful feedback and guidance.

Share experiences: Draw from your own experiences to provide real-world examples and insights. Sharing your successes and failures can offer valuable lessons and practical advice that resonates with your mentee.

Empower independence: While guidance is essential, empower your mentee to take ownership of their growth journey. Encourage them to explore, make decisions, and learn from their experiences.

Don't

Impose your path: Every individual's journey is unique. Refrain from imposing your personal career trajectory onto your mentee. Instead, help them identify and pursue their own path.

Disregard boundaries: Respect the boundaries set by your mentee. Be mindful of their time constraints, preferences, and comfort levels. Avoid overwhelming them with unsolicited advice or frequent communications.

Dismiss emotions: Acknowledge the emotional aspects of a mentee's journey. Whether they're facing challenges, doubts, or setbacks, be empathetic and provide a supportive space for them to share their feelings.

Offer unrealistic promises: Avoid making grandiose promises or guarantees of success. Mentorship is about guidance and growth, not instant solutions. Be realistic in your expectations and emphasize the importance of perseverance and continuous learning.

Effective mentorship requires a delicate balance of guidance, support, and respect. By adhering to these mentor do's and don'ts, you can foster a mentorship dynamic that empowers your mentee to achieve their goals, develop their skills, and navigate their professional journey with confidence. Your influence can have a profound impact on their success, so approach your role with the utmost care and dedication.

▩   ▩   ▩

The rest of this chapter and the following chapter is applicable for all mentors. Whether you're mentoring a new entrepreneur or someone navigating the corporate landscape, the following approaches will help you feel confident in how you're presenting as a mentor and aiding in their growth.

Mentoring beyond Pattern Matching: Nurturing Success across All Identities

Effective mentorship is about reaching across the spectrum of differences that define us, such as race, gender, and experiences. Mentoring individuals from various walks of life not only expands your own horizons but also brings fresh perspectives to your mentees. In return, as a mentor, you gain more than just a sense of fulfillment—you also

enhance your leadership and communication skills, which are essential for
your own career growth. Diverse mentorship accelerates promotions not
solely through vague concepts such as
soft skills but also by cultivating a rich
set of viewpoints and fostering understanding in a diverse world. In fact,
Cornell University's School of Indus-
trial and Labor Relations found that

*Diverse mentorship
accelerates promotions not
solely through vague concepts
such as soft skills but also by
cultivating a rich set of
viewpoints and fostering
understanding in a
diverse world.*

mentoring programs boosted minority representation at the management level by 9% to 24% (compared to −2% to 18% with other diversity initiatives).[1]

I experienced this personally. Transitioning from defense contracting to management consulting, I knew I would need a new group
of mentors.

Eight months into my career at a Big Four management consulting
firm, which was fully remote, I attended the firmwide marketing and
sales conference. This in-person event drew thousands of employees
keen on understanding the company's direction and expanding their
professional networks. At one of the receptions, I met Greg, a friendly
and approachable partner at the firm, although I didn't know his title
until we exchanged business cards later that night. Greg didn't let our
differences in career level, race, or gender identity act as barriers to
connecting. This was significant because many executives tend to
mentor individuals who share their gender or race.

I made a point to regularly discuss my career goals and progress
with Greg, who had been with the firm for over 25 years and had a
wealth of knowledge to share. He helped me align my career objectives
with the firm's direction and shared how he had maintained a strong
career path. When I expressed my entrepreneurial aspirations, he gave
me valuable feedback on The Mentor Method and how it could benefit
executives like him. His insights were instrumental in shaping the
platform's first iterations.

Greg's guidance also gave me the confidence to apply for the Mass-
Challenge Accelerator in Austin, Texas, a highly regarded business
accelerator program. I'm grateful for the path Greg helped me forge
into entrepreneurship.

As a mentor, you can have a profound impact on someone's life just like Greg did for me. By looking past superficial differences and focusing on potential, you open up a world of growth opportunities, both within your organization and in the broader community.

Mentoring at Work and in Your Community

There are two distinct paths that often emerge, when mentoring another professional—the mentorship that develops at work and the mentorship that develops outside of work through your community or professional associations. Both avenues offer unique opportunities for growth, learning, and impact, but they also come with their own set of dynamics, benefits, and potential risks.

Mentoring at Work

In the workplace, career mentorship takes on a structured and goal-oriented nature. It often involves pairing seasoned professionals with individuals who are navigating the same industry or organization. The mentor's experience provides insights, advice, and direction to help the mentee progress in their career trajectory. Mentees will seek guidance on navigating the intricacies of their roles, understanding organizational dynamics, and honing skills specific to their job functions.

One of the key benefits of workplace mentoring is the direct impact on an individual's job performance and career. The mentorship relationship overlaps with the mentee's daily responsibilities, allowing for real-time guidance that can result in immediate outcomes for them and the business. From refining technical skills to learning internal vernacular for effective internal communications, the workplace mentorship setting enables mentees to immediately apply insights gained from their mentor.

However, this space is not without its challenges. The risks lie in the potential for the mentorship relationship to become transactional or too company-centric, overshadowing the deeper growth that occurs when personal development is also nurtured. Striking the balance between skill enhancement and holistic growth can be a delicate task. Additionally, workplace dynamics and hierarchies may create power imbalances that need to be carefully navigated to ensure an equitable mentoring relationship.

Mentoring Outside of Work

Outside the boundaries of the workplace, mentorship takes on a more holistic and well-rounded approach. These mentorship relationships may come from diverse fields and backgrounds, offering insights that transcend the immediate day-to-day of your role as a mentor.

Mentoring outside of work allows for a more comprehensive exploration of an individual's aspirations, dreams, and challenges. This setting can encompass a range of scenarios, from mentoring a friend pursuing a different career path to guiding someone you connected with at an event through launching a new project. Your insights can help them make informed decisions about career changes, work-life balance, and personal aspirations. The rapport you build in this context often leads to deeper, more meaningful connections that can expand outside of standard work requirements.

The beauty of mentoring beyond work lies in its potential to tap into the mentee's core values and passions. As a mentor, you have the opportunity to inspire and encourage growth that extends far beyond a job description. The insights you share can influence not just career success but also overall life satisfaction and fulfillment.

The beauty of mentoring beyond work lies in its potential to tap into the mentee's core values and passions. As a mentor, you have the opportunity to inspire and encourage growth that extends far beyond a job description.

However, mentoring someone outside of work also presents risks. Without the boundaries and frameworks provided by the workplace, mentoring relationships outside of work may lack structure, leading to ambiguity or a lack of accountability. The line between mentorship and personal advice can blur, potentially leading to misunderstandings or unintended consequences. Additionally, addressing sensitive topics requires a high degree of empathy and emotional intelligence, as you navigate the complexities of your mentees' lives beyond work.

In both contexts, the role of mentor carries an inherent responsibility. Whether you're guiding a mentee toward a promotion within the organization or helping them navigate life choices, your influence is far-reaching. It's a testament to the profound impact you can have on another person's journey.

In the upcoming chapter, we'll take these fundamental principles and apply them to create a mentorship approach tailored to your unique qualities. This approach will not only make for an effective mentoring relationship, benefiting all parties, but it will also ensure that your experience as a mentor is enjoyable and fulfilling.

13

Crafting Your Authentic Mentor Identity for a Fulfilling Experience

AFTER A SPEAKING engagement for a Fortune 500 company, a woman approached me, seeking advice on how to become an effective mentor. Her initial words caught my attention as she hesitated, saying, "I don't think I'm mentor material." I couldn't resist the opportunity to understand what she meant by this statement.

I asked, "What makes you think you're not mentor material?" Her response highlighted a concern I had encountered countless times before—the perception that being a mentor requires conforming to a rigid, predetermined mold. It seemed that the advice she had received in the past left her feeling that she had to squeeze into a specific shape that simply didn't fit who she was.

Listening to her story, I found myself transported back to my own corporate journey, where I, too, experienced the weight of external expectations, which pushed me to conform to a predefined image that was never meant for me. It was at that moment that I felt a strong desire to set the record straight. Being a mentor is not about fitting into someone else's mold; it's about embracing your unique qualities and experiences.

> Being a mentor is not about fitting into someone else's mold; it's about embracing your unique qualities and experiences.

The truth is, as a mentor, you possess a distinctive opportunity to shape your mentoring style to fit your individuality. In the previous chapter, we laid down the foundational principles of what it takes to be a mentor. In this chapter, we'll take those fundamentals and, together with your self-awareness, craft a mentorship experience that is genuinely your own. After all, mentorship is about authenticity and tailoring your guidance to the specific needs and aspirations of your mentee.

Taking the Pressure Off to Enjoy the Process

Mentorship can be a deeply rewarding and delightful experience for mentors when you find the right balance that fits seamlessly into your life. For a fulfilling experience, align mentorship with your passions and interests. Mentoring in areas that genuinely excite you transforms the responsibility into an opportunity to share your expertise.

First, establish realistic expectations and boundaries. Your life, career, and goals continue to thrive alongside your mentoring role. Find a mentorship rhythm that suits your schedule without overwhelming it. Remember, the quality of your mentorship holds more weight than the quantity, so dedicate time you can comfortably commit to.

> Mentorship is not about leading your mentee; rather, it's about offering advice and sharing relevant experiences to help them reach their goals authentically. You don't need to know how to solve all your mentees' targeted growth areas or have your life completely figured out to engage with your mentees.

Mentorship is not about leading your mentee; rather, it's about offering advice and sharing relevant experiences to help them reach their goals authentically. You don't need to know how to solve all your mentees' targeted growth areas or have your life completely figured out to engage with your mentees. Prioritize authenticity, transparency, and a willingness to share your learning experiences, along with recommending resources or making introductions based on your discussions. Ultimately, your mentee is responsible for deciding how to incorporate this knowledge into their journey. By understanding yourself and asking thoughtful questions, you can determine if you are the best fit for their current aspirations.

Lastly, your honesty and openness about your uncertainties will strengthen your relationship with your mentee, who is likely facing similar pressures to have their entire career path mapped out. Keep the mentorship interactive and engaging. Mentorship should be a two-way street, where the exchange of ideas and insights enriches the journey for both parties.

Mentorship is a pathway to personal and professional growth, building meaningful relationships, and creating a positive impact on someone's life. Approach it with enthusiasm and authenticity, and it becomes an enriching part of your journey.

Declining a mentorship opportunity doesn't mean you won't mentor that person or anyone else in the future. It shows respect for the individual and acknowledgment of your current life stage, indicating that now may not be the best time. Alternatively, consider offering a one-time informational meeting to share insights without committing long-term. While leaders may feel pressured to accept mentorship requests, declining is often the most respectful course of action when you can't fully commit.

Your "Superhero Origin Story" Moment

Understanding your "superhero origin story" moment is a foundational aspect of becoming a mentor. This moment illuminates what drives your passion and explains why you are dedicated to mentorship. I unveiled my own "superhero origin story" moment in Chapter 2, which was a pivotal realization that fueled my desire to cultivate stronger mentor relationships. My initial career experiences underscored that conforming to a predefined mold or diminishing oneself to fit the corporate landscape was counterproductive. This revelation propelled me to encourage mentees to wholly embrace their authentic selves as a pivotal aspect of their career planning.

Your "superhero origin story" might stem from a significant life event or a moment of clarity that reshaped your perspective on mentorship. Identifying this moment provides direction and motivation in your mentoring role. It shapes your identity as a mentor and ensures your guidance aligns with your core motivations. Sharing this narrative with mentees may encourage them to discover their own origin stories, harness their strengths, and achieve their professional goals.

As a mentor, revisiting your defining "superhero origin story" moment helps maintain focus on the impact you aspire to create. It serves as a reminder of your dedication to sharing your time and expertise through mentorship, highlighting the value of enabling others to forge their unique professional paths. This shared pursuit of growth and discovery is what makes mentorship a rewarding and profound experience for both mentors and mentees.

Mentoring through Self-Awareness

Aligning your mentorship style with your unique identity as a mentor is an effective way to enhance the experience for both you and your mentees. As highlighted in Chapter 2, where mentees are encouraged to practice self-awareness, mentors should similarly reflect on their characteristics. Embracing your individual mentoring style not only helps in identifying mentees who are the right fit but also offers a deeper understanding of yourself, challenging preconceived notions and contributing to a fulfilling career path.

Explore your communication style, your views on workplace culture and career progression, seemingly minor details such as your preference for mornings or evenings, your stance on remote work or office presence, your favored team dynamics, and your proficiency in various industry sectors. Acknowledging these individual attributes will guide you toward selecting mentees who you can optimally support in a manner that resonates with you, thereby building a stronger relationship.

Questions for Self-Assessment

1. How do I prefer to communicate and interact with others in a professional context?

2. What beliefs and attitudes do I hold about workplace dynamics and career advancement?

3. Am I more energized in the mornings or evenings, and how does this affect my approach to work?

4. Do I support remote working and travel, or do I lean toward traditional office settings?

5. With what kind of teams do I perform best, and which environments are less conducive to my productivity?

6. In which sectors do I possess considerable knowledge and can provide meaningful mentorship?

7. Who were the memorable mentors in my career, and how have they influenced my path?

8. How has their mentorship influenced my growth and choices?

9. Do I recognize that mentorship involves sharing experiences and support rather than supplying all the answers?

10. Am I ready to engage with my mentee in a way that is genuine, open, and accepting?

What Type of Mentor Are You? For Professional Career Mentors

In your role as a mentor, you hold a unique position within your mentee's network of mentors. This network comprises a carefully selected group of leaders who collectively contribute to the holistic development of your mentee's career. Your participation as a mentor depends on your industry and your level of engagement in mentorship. You may find yourself filling one of the key mentorship roles that professionals need throughout their career journey.

In Chapter 3, we introduced seven mentor types that provide value at different career phases. Without realizing it, your mentee might view you as fitting one of these roles. To enhance your mentoring and foster meaningful discussions with your mentee, we'll examine each of these categories. This will also assist you in determining your position within your mentee's wider mentor network.

Company Insider

- The mentee frequently asks questions about company culture, office dynamics, and navigating internal politics.

- During discussions, the mentee seeks advice on aligning their goals with the organization's objectives.
- The mentee is interested in understanding the unwritten rules and norms within the company.
- They inquire about strategies to advance within the organization, showing a desire to progress within its framework.
- The mentee focuses on topics related to career growth within the company, such as mentor's personal experiences in achieving advancement.

How to Support Your Mentee as a Company Insider Mentor

- Provide context: Offer guidance on company culture, unwritten norms, and ways to navigate office dynamics.
- Guide on politics: Offer advice on handling office politics and building relationships within the organization.
- Facilitate connections: Introduce them to key stakeholders and colleagues to expand their network within the organization.
- Setting expectations: Help them align their goals with the company's objectives, and provide guidance on realistic expectations.
- Offer perspective: Share personal experiences of climbing the corporate ladder, emphasizing the importance of persistence and patience.
- Navigate challenges: Assist in overcoming internal challenges and finding solutions to issues unique to the company.

Skill Master

- The mentee seeks guidance on honing specific skills relevant to the mentor's expertise.
- Discussions revolve around improving areas such as public speaking, project management, or other skills that the mentor excels in.
- The mentee asks for resources, recommended courses, or practical tips to enhance their skill set.
- They express a desire to improve in certain professional domains and inquire about the mentor's journey in developing those skills.
- The mentee's questions are centered on practical strategies for applying and refining the specific skill.

How to Support Your Mentee as a Skill Master Mentor

- Personalized support: Tailor advice to their skill development needs, offering specific guidance and actionable steps.
- Resource recommendations: Suggest relevant workshops, courses, and materials that can aid in their skill development.
- Real-world application: Share real examples from your experiences and guide them on applying skills in practical scenarios.
- Practice opportunities: Offer practice sessions or mock scenarios to help them refine their skills in a safe environment.
- Structured feedback: Provide constructive feedback and suggestions to enhance their skill set effectively.
- Goal setting: Help them set clear goals for skill improvement and monitor their growth over time.

The Money-Minded Mentor

- The mentee initiates conversations about salary negotiations, promotions, and overall career progression.
- They ask for insights on strategies to increase earning potential and navigate compensation discussions.
- The mentee seeks advice on how to leverage achievements for better compensation and career advancement.
- Discussions involve sharing personal financial goals and seeking guidance on aligning career choices with financial aspirations.
- The mentee's focus on career growth and financial success is evident through their questions and engagement.

How to Support Your Mentee as a Money-Minded Mentor

- Salary negotiation strategy: Help them prepare for salary discussions, sharing tips on research, timing, and negotiation tactics. Coach them on effective negotiation techniques for salary discussions and promotions.
- Negotiation role play: Conduct role-playing exercises to simulate negotiation scenarios, helping them build confidence.
- Promotion road map: Guide them in creating a strategic plan for promotions, highlighting the skills and accomplishments needed.

- Long-term vision: Assist in setting financial goals aligned with their career aspirations, and offer advice on achieving them.
- Value proposition: Help them articulate their value to the organization and demonstrate their contributions.
- Case studies: Share success stories of individuals who successfully advanced in their careers by strategically negotiating.

The Industry Mentor

- The mentee's interest is more on the broader industry where you possess expert experience, rather than on a particular company.
- The mentee shows a keen interest in staying updated on industry trends, challenges, and opportunities.
- They seek advice on how to position themselves effectively within the industry.
- Conversations often revolve around understanding industry-specific best practices.
- The mentee inquires about the mentor's experiences and how they navigated challenges in the same industry.

How to Support Your Mentee as an Industry Mentor

- Industry insights: Keep them updated on the latest trends, advancements, and news within the industry.
- Career pathways: Offer guidance on different career trajectories within the industry, helping them set clear goals.
- Thought leadership: Encourage them to share their insights and expertise through thought leadership platforms.
- Informed decisions: Assist in making informed career decisions by providing context and industry-specific perspectives.
- Navigating changes: Offer guidance on adapting to shifts in the industry landscape and capitalizing on emerging opportunities.
- Industry challenges: Discuss common challenges and provide strategies for overcoming them based on your experiences.
- Networking introductions: Facilitate connections with industry professionals who can provide valuable insights and advice.
- Stay competitive: Advise them on continuous learning, certifications, and skills required to stay competitive in the industry.

The Network Mentor

- The mentee asks for advice on expanding their professional network and making professional connections for long-term goals.
- Conversations often revolve around strategies for effective networking and relationship building.
- The mentee seeks guidance on how to maintain and nurture professional connections over time.
- They inquire about the mentor's networking experiences and success stories.
- The focus of discussions is on building a robust network that supports career growth.

How to Support Your Mentee as a Network Mentor

- Networking strategy: Share effective networking strategies, both online and offline, that align with their goals.
- Introductions: Make introductions to your own network, opening doors to potential mentors, collaborators, and contacts.
- Event recommendations: Suggest relevant events, conferences, and workshops where they can expand their network.
- Follow-up guidance: Teach them the art of maintaining and nurturing connections over time for long-term relationships.
- Elevator overview coaching: Help them craft a concise and engaging elevator overview, described in Chapter 5, to make memorable first impressions.

The Influential Ally

- The mentee approaches the mentor for advice on navigating challenging situations or biases within the workplace.
- The mentee mentions admiration for your brand as a leader and influencer in your field, company, or professional association.
- Discussions often involve seeking guidance on leveraging allies to advance in their career.
- They inquire about strategies to enter into meetings, leadership committees, or projects where there is a perceived bias across age, race, gender identity, or socioeconomic access.

- The mentee seeks insights on how to align with influential advocates to amplify their professional impact.
- Conversations showcase the mentee's interest in leveraging allies to achieve career success and workplace equity.

How to Support Your Mentee as an Influential Ally Mentor

- Advocacy guidance: Offer advice on how to utilize your influence to support them in circles where you have sway.
- Equity and inclusion: Assist in overcoming workplace challenges related to bias and fostering diversity.
- Cultural sensitivity: Encourage appreciation of cultural variety and mentor in creating an inclusive work culture.
- Achievement celebrations: Acknowledge and celebrate their successes, professionally and otherwise.
- Leadership development: Supply tools and knowledge for developing leadership capabilities and becoming influential leaders.
- Career growth allyship: Help pinpoint and pursue opportunities that can propel the mentee's career forward using your influence.

Peer Mentor

- The mentee possesses one to three years less experience than you in your current role.
- The mentee seeks relatable advice and insights from the mentor, who has recently experienced similar situations.
- Conversations often revolve around practical approaches to overcoming obstacles faced at the mentee's career stage.
- The mentee inquires about the mentor's experiences and lessons learned during the same phase.

How to Support Your Mentee as a Peer Mentor

- Share experiences: Openly discuss your own experiences, challenges, successes, and lessons learned at their career stage.
- Practical advice: Offer practical solutions based on your recent experiences to help them navigate similar situations.
- Listening ear: Be an empathetic listener and provide emotional support as they face professional challenges.

- Joint learning: Suggest joint learning opportunities such as workshops or courses that align with their career stage.
- Resource sharing: Provide helpful resources, articles, and tools that aided you during your career progression.
- Goal alignment: Help them set achievable goals and milestones based on your own experiences.
- Encouragement and motivation: Offer continuous support, encouragement, and motivation as they navigate their professional journey.

▣ ▨ ▧

Within these mentorship categories, the mentee's questions, areas of focus, and the overall direction of their discussions serve as indicators of how they perceive their mentor's expertise and where they see them fitting into their career journey. The beauty of this process is that the mentee naturally guides the mentor to the category where they're most beneficial. In doing so, mentors then offer tailored support, supplying their mentees with the invaluable insights and guidance they need for their professional development.

What Type of Mentor Are You? For Entrepreneur Mentors

Early-stage entrepreneurs are in a dynamic and critical phase, turning ideas into viable businesses. They face uncertainties and limited resources, needing mentors with entrepreneurial experience to guide them.

In mentoring these individuals, your mentee may see you as one of the eight mentor types described in Chapter 11. Similar to the seven professional mentor roles, we'll examine these eight categories to better prepare you for these roles and clarify your position in your mentee's network of mentors.

The Industry Expert Mentor

- Your mentee's customer base may align with your current role. For example, if they sell their product or service to human resource professionals and you are a human resource executive.

- Your mentee asks detailed questions about industry trends, market shifts, and emerging technologies.
- They seek your guidance on navigating market challenges, customer preferences, and competitive dynamics.
- Your mentee asks about compliance, regulations, and legal considerations specific to your industry.
- They inquire about effective sales techniques, negotiation strategies, and understanding customer needs within your specific industry.
- Your mentee seeks introductions to key industry players and networking events.

How to Support Your Mentee as an Industry Expert Mentor

- Market insights: Share valuable industry trends, market dynamics, and emerging opportunities to help your mentee stay ahead.
- Networking connections: Introduce them to key players, potential collaborators, and industry events to expand their network.
- Regulatory guidance: Provide clarity on industry regulations and compliance standards to ensure their business operations are aligned.
- Strategic planning: Assist in crafting strategies that leverage your industry knowledge for better decision-making.
- Problem solving: Offer solutions to challenges specific to their industry, leveraging your experience to help them navigate obstacles.

The Fundraising and Investment Mentor

- Your mentee is preparing to raise funding for their business in the next 6–12 months.
- Your mentee seeks advice on creating a compelling pitch, identifying potential investors, and securing funding.
- They ask for connections to potential investors and seek guidance on crafting a persuasive pitch.
- Your mentee inquires about financial projections, valuation, and investment terms.
- They seek guidance on preparing for investor due diligence and building a strong investment case.

How to Support Your Mentee as a Fundraising and Investment Mentor

- Pitch deck refinement: Help them fine-tune their pitch deck, ensuring it effectively communicates their business value and vision.
- Investor introductions: Connect them with potential investors, VC firms, or angel investors from your network. _
- Investment strategy: Provide insights into different funding options, and guide them through the fundraising process.
- Financial projection review: Assist in creating realistic financial projections that align with investor expectations.
- Due diligence guidance: Prepare them for investor due diligence, helping them anticipate and address investor inquiries.

The Efficiency and Leadership Mentor

- Your mentee asks about streamlining operations, optimizing processes, and reducing costs.
- They seek advice on scaling the business, expanding to new markets, and managing growth.
- Your mentee inquires about hiring, building a high-performing team, and fostering a positive work culture.
- They seek guidance on leadership skills, conflict resolution, and effective communication.
- Your mentee values insights on unconventional growth strategies and creative problem solving.

How to Support Your Mentee as an Efficiency and Leadership Mentor

- Operational strategies: Offer techniques for optimizing business processes, increasing efficiency, and managing resources effectively.
- Scaling guidance: Provide a road map for scaling their business sustainably, while maintaining quality and customer satisfaction.
- Leadership development: Help them develop leadership skills, create a positive workplace culture, and inspire their team.
- Problem-solving approaches: Share your experience in overcoming growth challenges, offering actionable solutions.

- Change management: Guide them through periods of growth and change, helping them navigate transitions smoothly.

Financial Mentor

- Your mentee asks questions about bootstrapping their business while managing personal financial obligations.
- Your mentee asks about pricing strategies for their business.
- Your mentee asks for guidance on financial forecasting, budgeting, and managing cash flow.
- They seek advice on securing funding, managing investor relations, and optimizing financial resources.
- Your mentee inquires about making informed business investment decisions and evaluating ROI.
- They seek guidance on mitigating financial risks and ensuring financial stability.
- Your mentee values insights on exit planning, valuation, and acquisition opportunities.

How to Support Your Mentee as a Financial Mentor

- Financial planning: Assist in creating a comprehensive financial plan that aligns with their business goals and growth strategy.
- Funding navigation: Provide guidance on securing funding, preparing financial documentation, and engaging with investors.
- Budgeting expertise: Help them develop and manage budgets, ensuring their financial resources are allocated effectively.
- Financial decision support: Offer insights into financial decision-making, risk assessment, and investment prioritization.
- Cash flow management: Provide strategies to manage cash flow, optimize working capital, and achieve financial stability.

Peer Mentor

- Your mentee's business is one to three years behind your current business.

- Your mentee seeks advice on challenges specific to your stage of business growth.
- They ask for tools, resources, and strategies that help you overcome similar obstacles.
- Your mentee inquires about how you tackled challenges, made decisions, and learned from mistakes.
- They seek insights on setting achievable milestones and navigating common entrepreneurial hurdles.
- Your mentee values your encouragement and the relatability of your experiences.

How to Support Your Mentee as a Peer Mentor

- Stage-specific advice: Share experiences and strategies that are directly relevant to their current stage of business growth.
- Resource recommendations: Provide tools, resources, and practical advice that helped you overcome similar challenges.
- Realistic expectations: Set expectations based on your experiences, helping them navigate the ups and downs of entrepreneurship.
- Personal connection: Offer empathetic support by understanding the unique challenges they're facing as a peer.

The Technical or Product Mentor

- Your technical expertise is a clear lacking component for the entrepreneur or on their team.
- Your mentee seeks advice on technical implementation, software development, or product enhancement.
- They ask for guidance on improving technical skills, learning new technologies, and staying updated.
- Your mentee inquires about ways to innovate their product or leverage technology for business growth.
- They value your insights on approaching technical challenges and finding optimal solutions.
- Your mentee appreciates introductions to tech experts and relevant communities.

How to Support Your Mentee as a Technical or Product Mentor

- Skill enhancement: Provide guidance on technical skill development, recommending relevant courses and resources.
- Technology selection: Assist in choosing the right technology stack or tools that align with their business needs.
- Solution-oriented approach: Help them troubleshoot technical challenges and find practical solutions.
- Implementation guidance: Offer step-by-step guidance for implementing complex technical solutions in their business.
- Innovation insights: Share emerging technologies and trends that could drive innovation in their products or services.

The Brand and Marketing Mentor

- Your mentee seeks brand strategy guidance on defining their company brand identity, positioning, and differentiation.
- They ask for advice on creating marketing strategies, campaigns, and customer engagement.
- Your mentee inquires about building a strong online presence, social media strategies, and content marketing.
- They value insights on understanding customer behaviors, preferences, and market trends.
- Your mentee appreciates guidance on developing an executive presence and thought leadership.

How to Support Your Mentee as a Brand and Marketing Mentor

- Brand strategy development: Assist in crafting a strong brand identity, mission, and messaging that resonates with their target audience.
- Marketing campaign support: Provide guidance on creating effective marketing campaigns and measuring their impact.
- Online presence enhancement: Help them build a robust online presence through social media, content marketing, and SEO.
- Competitive analysis: Offer insights into their competitors' strategies, helping them identify unique selling points.
- ROI focus: Guide them in measuring the ROI of marketing efforts, ensuring their resources are used effectively.

- Personal brand development: Help them craft their personal brand alignment to the company's brand.

Personal Development Mentor

- Your mentee seeks advice on balancing work, personal life, and self-care.
- They ask for strategies to enhance focus, manage tasks efficiently, and achieve a fulfilling lifestyle.
- Your mentee inquires about setting meaningful goals, both personally and professionally.
- They value guidance on handling stress, overcoming challenges, and maintaining mental well-being.
- Your mentee appreciates recommendations on personal and professional skill development.

How to Support Your Mentee as a Personal Development Mentor

- Time management strategies: Share techniques for effectively managing time, prioritizing tasks, and maintaining work-life balance.
- Goal-setting techniques: Help them set short- and long-term goals and create action plans for personal and professional growth.
- Stress management: Offer strategies for managing stress and maintaining resilience in the face of challenges.
- Feedback and self-improvement: Guide them in seeking feedback, self-assessment, and continuous improvement.
- Networking tips: Provide advice on building meaningful connections, expanding their network, and fostering relationships.

▨ ▨ ▨

Given the dynamic pace of entrepreneurship, it's possible that you might find yourself mentoring within multiple categories, and these roles can change based on your mentee's evolving focus areas. This dynamism brings excitement to your role as a mentor, allowing you to engage with various aspects of your mentee's business and apply your own experiences to drive their entrepreneurial endeavors forward.

Exploring Your Mentorship Patterns

Taking a moment for a self-check-in can provide valuable insights into your mentorship patterns, highlight any potential blind spots, and help ensure you're prepared for the diverse landscape mentorship can present.

As a mentor, it's important to periodically pause and reflect on your experiences in mentorship. Taking a moment for a self-check-in can provide valuable insights into your mentorship patterns, highlight any potential blind spots, and help ensure you're prepared for the diverse landscape mentorship can present.

To evaluate your mentoring patterns for a more effective mentoring relationship, consider the following questions to ensure you're ready for the diverse situations mentorship may present.

1. Who have I been mentoring? Reflect on the individuals you've mentored, noting any patterns in their profiles. What does this suggest about areas you may be overlooking in your mentorship?

2. What are my ideas of a "good" mentee? Consider whether you've set specific expectations for selecting a mentee and how this may narrow your selection.

3. Is my mentorship industry specific? Consider if your focus on a certain career path or industry could be hindering a broader understanding of other sectors.

4. What are my beliefs about mentorship? Think about your assumptions regarding the mentorship process and its influence on your approach.

5. Am I comfortable with diversity in mentorship? Assess your readiness to mentor individuals from varied backgrounds and cultures.

6. How do I structure mentorship? Think about your mentorship style—structured or flexible—and how this could affect meeting different mentees' needs.

7. What are my mentoring strengths and weaknesses? Identify your areas of expertise and those that need improvement and consider their impact on your mentoring.

8. Am I assuming my mentees' objectives? Reflect on whether you're projecting your goals onto your mentees rather than understanding theirs.

9. How do I foster communication? Evaluate whether your communication style allows for an open exchange with your mentees.

10. Am I learning from my mentees? Assess your openness to learning from your mentees to foster a mutually beneficial mentorship relationship.

Effective Communication and Meetings with Your Mentee

As in any significant relationship, communication is a critical component to fostering a connection with your mentee. In previous chapters, mentees discovered ways to structure meetings, inquire with potential mentors to assess compatibility with their objectives, and methods to maintain or adapt the relationship for a positive trajectory. Now, let's explore how you can partner with your mentee to establish communication norms that foster a sense of empowerment and mutual respect.

Let Your Mentee Drive

Your mentee is responsible for driving the direction of your relationship. This includes organizing meetings, follow-ups, and deciding what to work on. As the mentor, allow your mentee to lead the relationship through encouraging them to take the lead in conversations. Mentorship is a collaborative effort, and empowering them to guide discussions can foster a sense of ownership and proactivity in their personal and professional development.

Engaging in the Initial Meeting with Your Mentee

When someone expresses their desire for you to be their mentor, it's indeed a flattering proposition. However, during those early conversations where you and your mentee are getting to know each other, it's helpful to resist the temptation to oversell yourself or feel pressured to prove your worth as a mentor. Instead, focus on gauging whether there's a genuine connection. Are your conversations natural and enjoyable?

Is your mentee open to feedback and guidance? Do you feel at ease when talking to this person?

Refrain from pressuring yourself into an immediate commitment. Take a day to reflect on your feelings after the initial meeting.

To determine whether they're a good fit for your mentoring style, consider asking them questions that provide insights into their personality and goals. Ask about their interests outside of work, the projects they're currently working on, and their career aspirations. It can also be insightful to inquire about their "superhero origin story" moment, mentioned in Chapter 2 and the previous chapter. Be prepared to share more about yourself, including your journey, why you're passionate about your work, and the areas in which you enjoy mentoring. If this is your first time as a mentor or a relatively new experience, don't hesitate to communicate that as well.

Refrain from pressuring yourself into an immediate commitment. Take a day to reflect on your feelings after the initial meeting. If you don't find yourself eagerly looking forward to their follow-up meeting, feel drained by the thought of balancing your existing workload with mentorship, or are already contemplating ways to support them and connect them with valuable contacts and events, listen to your initial instincts. It's unlikely that these feelings will change, and they often reflect your genuine inclinations.

Preparation for Recurring Meetings with Your Mentee

Before your scheduled meetings, review the agenda provided by your mentee or inquire if there are specific topics they'd like to address during your interaction. This allows you to prepare mentally and consider how you can offer support without needing a rigid script. Simply anticipate the mindset you'll need to assist your mentee. Are they seeking tactical guidance for project execution, insights on how you achieved your recent promotion, or advice on skill development? Understanding their needs will make your meetings more productive and valuable.

Additionally, brainstorm questions that you may want to ask your mentee during the meetings. These questions can serve various purposes, such as helping you understand their objectives, aiding their thought processes, or guiding them toward their desired outcomes. A mentor might ask questions that lead the mentee to realize the answers to their own questions, fostering self-discovery and growth. Questions to promote self-discovery and growth include:

1. What are the specific objectives or milestones you're pursuing in your career, and what makes them significant to you?

2. Could you discuss a recent challenge you've faced professionally or in your self-improvement efforts? How do you plan to tackle it?

3. What approaches are you contemplating to enhance your skills and abilities? In which areas do you feel improvement is needed the most?

4. Have you come across any hurdles or uncertainties on your career journey? Let's discuss how we can collaboratively overcome these issues to define a more direct path.

5. Think about what your recent experiences and accomplishments have taught you. How will the lessons from your triumphs and setbacks inform your future projects?

Leveraging Your Network to Help Your Mentee

Consider involving additional resources to support your mentee's goals. Just as CEOs recognize the importance of assembling a specialized team to achieve various objectives, you too can contemplate who else might be a valuable resource for your mentee.

Let's consider Sarah, a dedicated mid-level manager at a prominent global tech company. She's a seasoned mentor, passionate about helping newcomers thrive in the tech industry, and is mentoring Reid, who recently joined the company. Reid was eager to develop his public speaking and presentation skills, which were needed for his role in client interactions and project pitches.

Sarah, though an excellent manager and mentor, was candid about her own struggle with public speaking. She recognized the importance of this skill but felt it wasn't her forte. Rather than letting her limitations hinder Reid's growth, she decided to provide him with a well-rounded learning experience.

Sarah began by having an open and honest conversation with Reid about her personal journey, explaining her efforts to improve her own public speaking abilities. She acknowledged her limitations and made it clear that while she would support him to the best of her abilities, she believed he could benefit from a broader perspective.

To ensure that Reid had access to the expertise he needed, Sarah connected him with a colleague, Mark, who was renowned in the company for his exceptional public speaking skills. Mark had presented at major tech conferences and was highly regarded as a proficient communicator.

With Sarah's recommendation, Reid reached out to Mark, and they started working together on developing his public speaking abilities. This additional mentorship provided Reid with insights, guidance, and practical techniques that complemented the foundational support he received from Sarah.

As a result, Reid's confidence in public speaking flourished, and his presentations became more compelling and engaging. Sarah's willingness to acknowledge her limitations and introduce Reid to a subject matter expert not only supported his growth but also reinforced her commitment to being a valuable mentor.

This example showcases how mentors can leverage their network and seek additional guidance for their mentees when addressing skills or topics beyond their own expertise, ultimately offering a more well-rounded learning experience.

Setting Clear Expectations and Healthy Boundaries with Your Mentee

Establishing clear expectations and healthy boundaries is a fundamental element of effective mentorship. While the eagerness to guide and support your mentee is natural, avoid the role of a "rescuer" as it can lead to over-involvement and potential challenges in your mentor-mentee relationship.

To strike the right balance, start by evaluating your existing personal and professional commitments before taking on a mentee. This self-assessment helps in setting realistic expectations regarding your availability and engagement level in the mentorship. Be up front about your preferred times for mentorship meetings, whether you manage your own schedule or have a designated contact for scheduling.

Another key factor in setting expectations is defining the communication channels that work best for both you and your mentee. Whether you prefer email, text messages, or scheduled calls, make it clear what the most effective means of staying connected are for you. It's just as important that you communicate the structure of the mentorship arrangement with your mentee so that expectations are managed. Clearly outline whether you have bandwidth for monthly, biweekly, or weekly meetings, or follow another schedule. This ensures that both you and your mentee share a common understanding of the commitment and the frequency of interactions.

When it comes to determining the scope of your mentorship, specifying your availability and preferences from the beginning is key. This proactive approach minimizes the chances of future misunderstandings or conflicts.

By setting these clear expectations and boundaries, you lay a strong foundation for a productive and mutually beneficial mentorship relationship. This approach not only prevents potential communication issues but also enables you to offer meaningful support to your mentee without compromising other areas of your life.

⬛ ⬜ ⬛

Crafting your mentor identity is a thoughtful and intentional process that prepares you to support your mentees effectively. By tapping into your distinctive strengths and understanding the best ways to assist your mentees, you set the stage for a fulfilling mentorship role.

Expertise in every area isn't necessary; what's important is your willingness to impart wisdom, engage in active listening, and guide your mentees toward their goals. This approach promotes their growth and enhances your own capabilities.

Developing as a mentor is a continuous path of personal growth, contribution, and influential connections. It's about nurturing growth and making a lasting, positive impact on your mentees' lives. As you evolve in this role, you'll discover that mentorship is a deeply rewarding experience that benefits you just as much as those you mentor. Stay authentic, embrace your unique self, and enjoy the enriching path of mentorship.

Thank You for Mentoring

I would like to express my sincere appreciation for your commitment to becoming a mentor. Transitioning to a mentoring role represents a significant change in mindset, signifying your dedication and the willingness to share the lessons learned from the considerable effort you've put into your personal and professional development. It's a notable step to now be in a position to contribute, motivate, and mentor others.

As you embrace this new role, you reflect the principles of servant leadership, sharing your wisdom and resources selflessly. This nurturing approach is the hallmark of effective mentorship, and you are precisely the mentor that is needed today.

I recognize the ongoing commitment this journey entails and the positive influence you will have on your mentees. As you guide their careers, know that you are fostering a legacy that extends beyond individual success, contributing to a collective advancement. Your choice to mentor speaks volumes of your dedication to growth—both personal and shared—and for that, I thank you deeply.

Conclusion

As YOU REACH the conclusion of this book, you find yourself at a crossroads filled with opportunities. Your journey has been rich with self-discovery, skill enhancement, and a deeper comprehension of mentorship's comprehensive impact. So what's your next step?

The answer has two parts: mentorship and integration. Having witnessed the transformative power of mentorship, consider stepping up to become a mentor yourself. No matter where you are in your career, your experiences and insights are deeply valuable to those aspiring to follow in your footsteps. Acting as a peer mentor can set off a ripple of positive change, building a community of individuals dedicated to supportive growth.

Extend your reach by promoting this model of mentorship among your friends and colleagues. Encourage them to start their own journeys, embracing self-acceptance, self-development, and forming meaningful mentor-mentee relationships that can propel their careers forward. In sharing this philosophy, you're contributing to a movement of empowerment that extends beyond the pages of this book.

Remember, mentorship isn't just for professional settings. Your internal transformation can have an effect on every aspect of your life. The knowledge you've acquired, the strategies you've honed, and the growth you've experienced all intertwine with the core of who you are.

> *The knowledge you've acquired, the strategies you've honed, and the growth you've experienced all intertwine with the core of who you are. Use this wisdom as you face challenges, chase dreams, and navigate the complexities of life.*

Use this wisdom as you face challenges, chase dreams, and navigate the complexities of life.

Take a moment to reflect on how far you've come. Celebrate your accomplishments and the obstacles you've overcome. As you stand at the brink of new beginnings, bear in mind that your journey is far from over. Let your enthusiasm be the fuel that drives you toward a career and lifestyle that align with your aspirations and truest self.

Harness the wisdom, the connections, and the newfound strength that have become pillars of your journey. With these tools, coupled with a strong mentorship network, you're well equipped to make significant strides in both your personal and professional life. As you turn the last page, let this book shine a light on the path ahead. May your story be a source of inspiration, a testament to the profound impact mentorship can have.

Congratulations on this momentous chapter in your life. The pages of this book are merely the opening act to the incredible narrative you'll craft in the years ahead. So step forward with confidence, intent, and the unwavering belief that you have the power to unlock your full potential.

Notes

Introduction

1. Pease, Gene, *Optimize Your Greatest Asset—Your People: How to Apply Analytics to Big Data to Improve Your Human Capital Investments*, APPENDIX E: "Mentoring Case Study," Wiley, 2015, https://doi.org/ https://onlinelibrary.wiley.com/doi/pdf/10.1002/9781119040002.app5.
2. Wronski, Laura, "Nine in 10 Workers Who Have a Career Mentor Say They Are Happy in Their Jobs," CNBC, July 16, 2019, https://doi.org/ https://www.cnbc.com/2019/07/16/nine-in-10-workers-who-have-a-mentor-say-they-are-happy-in-their-jobs.html.
3. Comaford, Christine, "76% Of People Think Mentors Are Important," *Forbes*, https://doi.org/https://www.forbes.com/sites/christinecomaford/2019/07/03/new-study-76-of-people-think-mentors-are-important-but-only-37-have-one/?sh=53c730043297.
4. Ibid.

Chapter 3

1. Gross, Christopher "CJ," "A Better Approach to Mentorship," *Harvard Business Review*, June 6, 2023, https://hbr.org/2023/06/a-better-approach-to-mentorship#:~:text=from%20marginalized%20communities.-,Research%20shows%20that%2071%25%20of%20executives%20choose%20to%20mentor%20employees,this%20becomes%20a%20big%20problem.

211

2. Timotic, Milos, "The Most Interesting Mentorship Statistics You Need to Know," Trafft, April 3, 2023, https://trafft.com/mentorship-statistics/.
3. Ibid.
4. Ibid.
5. "The State of Allyship Report: The Key to Workplace Inclusion," Empovia, n.d. empovia.co/allyship-report/.

Chapter 4

1. "Mentoring Relationships and Demographic Diversity," Military Leadership Diversity Commission, https://doi.org/https://diversity.defense.gov/Portals/51/Documents/Resources/Commission/docs/Issue%20Papers/Paper%2025%20-%20Mentoring%20Relationships%20and%20Demographic%20Diversity.pdf.
2. Dimmock, Liz, "New UK Research: Mentoring Is Improving Gender Balance in Organisations," Moving Ahead, September 7, 2017, https://doi.org/https://www.women-ahead.org/press/turning-the-dial.

Chapter 7

1. Beecham, Amy, "The Stack World Conference: CEO Sharmadean Reid on Why Every Woman Should Have a Mentor at Work," Stylist, September 17, 2022. https://doi.org/https://www.forbes.com/sites/nazbeheshti/2019/01/23/improve-workplace-culture-with-a-strong-mentoring-program/www.stylist.co.uk/life/careers/sharmadean-reid-the-stack-world-conference-mentorship/715387.

Chapter 11a

1. Timotic, Milos, "The Most Interesting Mentorship Statistics You Need to Know," Trafft, April 3, 2023, https://trafft.com/mentorship-statistics/.

Chapter 12

1. "Improve Workplace Culture with a Strong Mentoring Program," *Forbes*, January 23, 2019, www.forbes.com/sites/nazbeheshti/2019/01/23/improve-workplace-culture-with-a-strong-mentoring-program/.

Acknowledgments

I'M PROFOUNDLY GRATEFUL to my agents, Claire Friedman and Eliza Rothstein at InkWell Management, for their guidance, mentorship, patience, and for always encouraging me to think bigger.

To my editor, Victoria Savanh, her assistant, Trinity Crompton, and Wiley Publishing leadership, your insights and support have been instrumental in bringing this book to life. I appreciate the time and effort you've invested in my work.

Michelle Hacker, my managing editor, Julie Kerr, my developmental editor, and Dulari Gandhi, I cannot thank you enough. Julie, you were not just a developmental editor—your meticulous attention to detail is unparalleled.

To my parents, thank you for your prayers, wisdom, and the sacrifices you made to provide me with a life filled with opportunities and love. I am deeply indebted to the women in my family—your sacrifices, love, and encouragement have shaped me into the person I am today. To the women in my family who passed with stifled dreams, my voice is your voice. This achievement is as much yours as it is mine.

I'm deeply grateful to my author friends, who have been literary mentors, for generously sharing their insights and experiences with me throughout this journey. Your guidance helped me through every stage of the author process.

To my dearest friends, this section can't do justice to how grateful I am for you. Your presence has been a pillar of strength, and I am eternally grateful for each one of you. Every call, text, conversation, walk, and listening ear means more to me than I can articulate. Thank you for being my chosen family. I love you.

A special thank-you to Kim Scott, Hugh Forrest, Chris Hyams, Shellye Archambeau, Jan Ryan, Joseph Kopser, Kimberly Strong, and Chris Pacitti for reading early versions of the manuscript, believing in me, and helping to advance this book. Your wisdom is woven into these pages, and I hope you see this book as a reflection of the lessons I've learned from you. To Brené Brown, being a guest on your *Dare to Lead* podcast was a transformative experience that I will cherish forever. Your support has been invaluable to me.

I'm incredibly grateful for my therapist, Danielle Locklear, and my leadership coach, Genie Sockel, who have been instrumental in my personal and professional growth.

Lastly, and most importantly, thank you to everyone who has shared their mentorship and career stories with me. Your vulnerability and willingness to share your dreams, aspirations, wins, and losses have not only shaped this book but also me as a person. I carry your stories with me every day.

Index

Personal growth
gap, 5–6
identification, 16–18
Personal strengths, reflection, 17
Potential, unmasking, 12–13
Pressure, management, 15–16
Proactive communication, 96–97
Problem-solving skills, importance, 3
Professional career mentors, 189–195
Professional identity
discovery, tools, 11–12
embracing, 10
Professional relationship, maintenance, 57
Professional self, transformation, 9–10
Progress, tracking process, 18

Q
Qualities, uniqueness, 67

R
Relationships
building, expertise, 95
empathy, basis, 21
retirement, respect, 118–119
value, mentor expression, 20
Resilience, importance, 4
Reverse mentorship, 23
Risks, mitigation, 57
Role model, 25

S
Salary information (elevator overview exclusion), 63
Self-advocating check-in, 15
Self-assuredness, sense, 12
Self-awareness, 188–189
prioritization, 14
requirement, 15
transformative power, 7
Self-confidence, building, 21
Self-discovery, concept, 9
Self-insight, usage, 8–9

Self-reflection, 45
encouragement, 25
Skill development, mentorship (impact), 21
Skill master mentor, 41, 190–191
characteristics/roles, 30, 123, 126, 129, 132–133
questions, 31
usage, benefit, 27
Social media, mentorship connections, 54
Story, mentor list transformation, 52–53
Strengths/wins/achievements, ownership/embracing, 60–61
Superhero origin story, 12–13, 187–188

T
Technical or product mentor, 153–155, 199–200
questions, 154–155
role/characteristics, 153
Traditional mentorship, 23
Traits (elevator overview component), 62
True self, embracing (impact), 10

V
Value/vision, maximization, 139–140
Virtual environment, offers, 53
Vulnerability
mentorship, relationship, 21
requirement, 15

W
Work
mentoring, 182
mid-level experience, 122
network, exploration, 56–58
style, exploration, 10
Work-based relationship, personal life (avoidance), 56
Workforce, first-time entry, 122